Cooking with Merlot

75 Marvelous Merlot Recipes

by

Barbara and Norm Ray

Rayve Productions
Hoffman Press division

On the cover: Merlot grapes

Photograph: Jean-Pierre Huser
Cover design: Randall F. Ray
Interior illustrations: William J. Geer and A. Ariel

Rayve Productions Inc.
Hoffman Press division
Box 726, Windsor, CA 95492

Quantity discounts and bulk purchases of this and other Hoffman Press
books are available through Rayve Productions Inc. For more information
and to place orders call toll-free 1-800-852-4890 or fax 707-838-2220.

Library of Congress Cataloging-in-Publication Data

Ray, Barbara, 1941 -
    Cooking with merlot : 75 marvelous merlot recipes / by Barbara
    and Norm Ray.
      p.cm.
    Includes index.
    ISBN 1-877819-53-3 (alk. paper)
    1. Cookery (Wine) 2. Wine and wine making I. Ray, Norm II.
    Title

TX726.R37723 2003
641.6'22--dc21   2002036606

To Virginia and Bob,

who guided and encouraged us with their

. . . joie de vivre

. . . excellent recipes

and

. . . wise words

Introduction to Merlot

The word "Merlot" means "young blackbird" in French, probably alluding to this red wine grape's rich blue-black color. More precisely, the more popular varietal is "Merlot Noir" with its less-well-known sister variety being "Merlot Blanc." Merlot Noir is used in the recipes in this book.

The Merlot grape originated in southern France and Italy, was designated a distinct variety in the 1800s, and is now grown throughout the world. Soft and mellow, Merlot enhances the flavors of other grapes and has traditionally been used as a blending grape, but it is also an excellent wine in its own right, a fact Europeans have long appreciated. Americans, on the other hand, have discovered the pleasures of fine-quality Merlot only in recent decades, and its popularity is increasing throughout the United States.

Merlot wines vary widely in flavor, depth, and complexity, which are determined by the source appellation, viticultural area, vintage, winemaking techniques, and numerous other subtle factors. High-quality Merlot wines are medium to dark red in color, and complex with distinct nuances of fruit and fragrance – black cherry, black currant, plum, and others.

Merlot wines mature earlier and can be drunk earlier than many other red wines, but, generally speaking, they do not age as well. Because of this, wine makers sometimes blend a small amount of Cabernet Sauvignon or Cabernet Franc with Merlot grapes to give the wine more structure. A well-balanced Merlot may age well, but then again, it may not. Since most well-blended Merlots are rich, velvety and delicious when young, it's safer to buy and enjoy them at that time. However, if you do plan to store a favorite Merlot, be sure it's top quality because an excellent Merlot is likely to age well over a longer period of time, generally speaking from 2 to 5 years, and in some cases, longer.

When you're planning to cook moderately heavy cuisine, think Merlot. It is an excellent choice for soups, red meat, poultry, seafood, red pasta dishes, and desserts that contain red fruit or chocolate. And, of course, Merlot is the perfect accompaniment to these dishes, too.

Cooking with Wine Can Be Good for Your Health

You can reduce the amount of calories, sodium, fat and cholesterol dramatically when you cook with wine. Wine adds a richness to food that easily replaces high calorie ingredients. Using dessert as an example, fruit that is poached in wine and served with a cookie or two has less than half the calories of a slice of chocolate cake.

You may use less salt, too, when you cook with wine. Salt can be replaced by the flavorful nuances of the ingredients in the dish when combined with wine. It is also easy to reduce the amount of fats and oil that you use. In place of the usual butter, margarine or cooking oil, use a few drops of olive oil or a spritz or two of cooking oil to cook meat, poultry or fish, then use wine liberally to complete the cooking by poaching instead of frying.

When frying foods, you can easily make a sauce that will be a true gourmet's delight ... with fat and calories greatly reduced. Simply combine wine with the browned bits from the pan, and stir in a little flour to thicken the sauce.

Cholesterol levels, too, are greatly decreased and the natural goodness of your dish is enhanced when wine is used in place of cheese, cream, butter and fat.

It's nice to know that it is possible to eat well, drink well, and enjoy better nutrition, too, isn't it?

Cooking-with-Wine Basics

You can't cook well with bad wine. Nothing has ever been found that equals wine in cooking, but you can't cook well with bad wine. If a Merlot tastes vinegary, raw or unpleasant, throw it out. A small amount of bad wine can ruin a dish, just as one rotten apple can spoil a barrelful.

Cook with wine you enjoy. The most important guide in choosing a specific Merlot for your cooking is your taste buds. Although it's a good idea to review published wine evaluations and talk with wine experts about the various brands of Merlot, ultimately you should select a good-quality wine that tastes good to you. If you don't like the taste, don't use it! Cooking will not hide or enhance the flavor; in fact, it will intensify it. Knowing this, experienced cooks avoid cheap, poorly made wines.

You don't need expensive vintage wine for cooking. It is important to cook with a moderately priced *good-quality* wine, but not necessarily an expensive *great* wine. The rich subtleties of a great wine's bouquets and flavors, which are so enjoyable when sipping, may be lost or greatly diminished when blended with herbs, spices, and other cooking ingredients and subjected to heat. So, use the good-quality Merlot for your cooking, and serve the expensive vintage to accompany it.

Add the wine when the recipe calls for it. *When* you add the wine to the other ingredients is crucial. Don't add it too soon, or too late. Wine performs in certain ways under certain conditions. For example, a beef stew will usually call for the wine to be added early in the recipe so it can marinate the meat, blend with other seasonings, and evaporate its alcohol during cooking.

On the other hand, a soup or dessert may require that wine be added just before it is served to provide the whole flavor of the wine, which would be dispelled if cooked.

Add Merlot to suit your taste. When adding Merlot to your own recipes, begin with the following portions and add more wine as desired.

	<u>Quantity of Merlot Wine</u>
Soups	
Meat	1 teaspoon per portion
Vegetable	1 teaspoon per portion
Meats	
Beef, Lamb, Game	¼ cup per pound
Ham	2 cups (for basting)
Pastas	
Sauce	¼ cup per portion
Poultry	
Chicken, Turkey, roasted	½ cup per pound (for basting)
Chicken, poached	½ cup per pound (for basting)
Duck, Game Hen, Goose	¼ cup per pound (for basting)
Seafood (Add wine prior to cooking)	
Fish, broiled, baked, poached	¼ cup per pound
Fish, sautéed	4 tablespoons per pound
Shellfish	¼ cup per pound
Fruits & Vegetables	
Fresh Fruit	1 teaspoon per portion
Cooked Vegetables	1 teaspoon per portion
Salads	1 teaspoon per portion

Most important of all, enjoy yourself! We do, and we hope that you, too, will enjoy preparing the recipes in this book and creating new recipes using Merlot wines. Cooking with wine is a joyous adventure!

Barbara and Norm Ray

Serving Wine

Serving wine correctly adds class to any occasion. Following are tips to give you added confidence when serving your guests.

Temperature: Merlot and other red wines are best when served at temperatures of 57-68° F. Room temperature is rarely ideal. When too warm, chill bottles of Merlot in the refrigerator, ten minutes for every 4° F decrease in temperature, to about 57° F, which will allow for a little warming after wine is poured.

Wine glasses: Merlot tastes better in a stemmed wine glass with a fairly large, round bowl that has a minimum capacity of 8-17 ounces and a generous surface area to enhance the wine's bouquet. The glass should be clear to allow guests to examine the wine's color and body, and it should curve in at the top to retain the bouquet. Hold the glass by the stem to prevent heat from your hand warming the wine unless warmer wine is desired.

Pouring wine: Merlot should be poured towards the center of the glass. To prevent drips, twist the bottle slightly as you tilt it upright. Fill the glass to the widest part of the bowl, allowing room to swirl the wine and smell its bouquet. At a dinner party, serve wine to women and older guests first, then to men, and, finally, fill your own glass.

FRONT LABEL

(1)
(2)

Our Own Brand

1997

(3)
(4)

Reserve
Estate Bottled

(5)
(6)

Our Own Vineyard
The American Valley

(7)

Merlot

(8)

Net contents 750ml   13.5% alcohol

(9)

Vinted & bottled by Our Own Winery
Wineland, WV, USA

BACK LABEL

Vinted and Bottled by Our Own Winery, Wineland, WV, USA

(10)

Government warning: (1) According to the Surgeon General, women should not drink alcoholic beverages during pregnancy due to the risk of birth defects. (2) Consumption of alcoholic beverages impairs your ability to drive a car or operate machinery and may cause health problems. Contains sulfites.

(11)

The grapes for this wine were grown in our vineyards and vinted in our own winery by members of the same family that planted the original grape vines in 1835. We hope that you will enjoy this wine as much as we did in making it for you.

The Label on the Bottle

A wine bottle label, by law, must provide an accurate description of the wine. That is mandatory. But there is usually a great deal more on the label than that. Here is a guide to reading and understanding terms you'll find on wine bottle labels.

1. The brand name. These days one winery may produce multiple varieties of wines under different labels. Some are secondary lines of wines ... not necessarily inferior, but possibly with less aging, or tank fermented instead of barrel fermented, etc. Other labels may represent a new wine available only in limited quantities.

2. The date. If there is a date on the bottle, it refers to the year the grapes were harvested and the wine made from those grapes, not simply the year in which the wine was made. In the United States, the wine label may list the vintage year if 95 percent of the wine comes from grapes crushed that year.

3. Reserve. This is a term used, by choice, by some vintners to indicate something special about the wine. It may be great grapes, quality barrel aging, or other unique features.

4. Estate bottled. This term came from France where wineries were traditionally located where the vineyards were. In the United States, where many vineyards are miles away from the winery, "Estate Bottled" indicates that the winery either owns or controls the vineyard and is responsible for the growing of the grapes used in this bottle of wine.

5. The vineyard name. The vineyard name on a wine bottle label indicates that very high-quality grapes were used in the making of that wine. Vineyard designation is purely voluntary on the part of the winery.

6. The appellation. This is a legally protected name under which a wine may be sold, indicating that the grapes used are of a specific kind and are grown in a specific geographic area. By law, 85% of the grapes used in the production of the wine must come from that region.

7. The name of the wine. The wine name may be 1) a grape varietal, such as Chardonnay, Merlot, etc., 2) the name given by the winery to a specific blend of wines, such as Meritage, or 3) a simple proprietary name such as "Red Table Wine."

8. The size of the bottle and the alcohol content. The standard wine bottle is 750 ml. (25.4 oz.), a half bottle is 375 ml., and a split, or one-quarter bottle, is 187 ml. By law, American wines may not contain more than 14% alcohol by volume.

9. The name and address of the bottler.

10. Contains sulfites. Most wines contain sulphur dioxide, a preservative that is added to the wine. Listing all additives on the label is a legal requirement.

11. The message. Many wineries use back labels, too. Here you'll often find useful information about the wine, what flavors it embodies, foods it will pair well with, and other useful facts. Read the back label. It will be helpful in choosing the right wine for the right meal at the right price.

Contents

Soups

Chilled Tomato-Vegetable Soup

8	ripe tomatoes, blanched, peeled and seeded
2	English cucumbers, peeled and seeded
2	red bell peppers, peeled and seeded
1	stalk of celery, strings removed
¼	medium onion, peeled
½	jalapeño pepper, cored, seeded and finely chopped
½	serrano chili, cored, seeded and finely chopped
¼	cup Merlot wine
½	cup tomato juice
¼	cup olive oil
½	teaspoon sea salt or kosher salt
¼	teaspoon black pepper
¼	teaspoon cayenne pepper
2	tablespoons chopped fresh herbs (Italian parsley, chives, cilantro, tarragon)

Cut prepared tomatoes, cucumbers, bell peppers, celery, and onion into 1-inch pieces. Place them in a stainless steel bowl along with the jalapeño pepper and serrano chili. Add the Merlot wine, tomato juice, and olive oil. Season with the salt, black pepper, and cayenne pepper. Cover tightly and refrigerate overnight, stirring occasionally.

Place mixture in a food processor and, using the pulse setting, mince until the vegetables are fine but still have some texture to them. Return mixture to bowl and add the freshly chopped herbs. Correct the seasoning to taste. Chill well and serve in well-chilled bowls.

Serves 6

Serve with Merlot.

Mushroom-Merlot Bisque

1   **pound mushrooms, minced**
1½ **cups heavy cream**
6   **ounces clam juice (1 small bottle)**
2   **tablespoons minced shallots**
6   **fennel seeds**
4   **tablespoons butter**
4   **tablespoons flour**
3   **cups chicken stock**
¼   **teaspoon sea salt or kosher salt**
¼   **teaspoon fresh grated nutmeg**
2   **tablespoons Merlot wine**
     Fresh fennel for garnish

Chop the mushrooms in a food processor, in a meat grinder, or by hand with a knife until they are fine but still have some texture. Be careful not to overprocess them. Bring the mushrooms, cream, clam juice, minced shallots and fennel seeds to a boil and simmer for 10 minutes.

While the mushrooms are cooking, make a roux by melting the butter, allowing the foam to subside, and then stirring in the flour. Cook this mixture over low heat for 5 minutes, stirring frequently. Set aside to cool.

After the mushrooms have simmered 10 minutes, add the chicken stock, salt and nutmeg. Add a cup or so of this mixture to the cooled roux, stir smooth, then whisk back into the soup. Bring to a simmer and cook for 15 minutes. Stir in Merlot.

Garnish with sprigs of fennel and serve.

Serves 6

Serve with Merlot.

Hearty Lentil Soup

3	tablespoons olive oil
2	large onions, chopped
1	carrot, chopped
½	teaspoon dried marjoram
½	teaspoon dried thyme
1	teaspoon sea salt or kosher salt
½	teaspoon black pepper
3	cups beef stock
1	cup dry lentils, washed
1	14½-ounce can ready-cut tomatoes, undrained
¼	cup chopped fresh parsley
½	cup Merlot wine
¾	cup grated Sonoma jack or other jack cheese
3	strips bacon, cooked crisp and crumbled

In a large saucepan, heat the olive oil; sauté the onions and carrot for 3 to 5 minutes. Add the herbs, salt and pepper; sauté for 1 minute more. Add the stock, lentils, tomatoes with their juice, and the parsley.

Cover the saucepan and cook until the lentils are tender, 45 to 60 minutes. Add the Merlot. Taste for seasoning, adding more salt and pepper if necessary.

To serve, place 2 tablespoons grated cheese in each serving bowl, pour in soup and top with crumbled bacon. May be made ahead and reheated . . . it gets better.

Serves 4 to 6

Serve with Merlot.

Garlic-Onion Soup

2½   tablespoons butter
3   garlic cloves, minced
5   medium onions (about 1½ pounds), thinly sliced
¼   cup Merlot wine
¼   teaspoon dried thyme
¼   teaspoon dried rosemary
¼   teaspoon kosher salt
¼   teaspoon ground black pepper
1   quart chicken broth

CROUTONS
½   loaf French bread, four 1-inch slices, cut on diagonal
5   tablespoons olive oil
¼   cup Merlot wine
3   ounces Swiss cheese, thinly sliced
½   cup grated Parmesan cheese

In a large, deep skillet, melt butter. Add garlic and onions; cover and cook over medium heat, stirring occasionally, until soft, about 7 minutes. Uncover and sauté until golden, about 5 minutes longer. Add Merlot wine, herbs, salt, pepper and chicken broth. Bring to a boil. Cover, reduce heat, and simmer for about 5 minutes.

To make croutons, heat 3 tablespoons of the olive oil in a large skillet. Add bread and sauté on both sides until light brown, about 2 minutes. Drizzle with Merlot and remaining oil, and top with Swiss cheese slices. Cover and cook over medium heat until cheese melts, 2 to 3 minutes. Place croutons on individual servings of soup and sprinkle with Parmesan cheese.

Serves 4

Serve with Merlot.

Seafood Chowder with Merlot

½	cup olive oil
2	cloves garlic, minced
2	small scallions, minced
½	pound very ripe Roma tomatoes, peeled and diced, or 1 cup canned tomato juice
1	medium carrot, diced
1	stalk celery, minced
3	tablespoons fresh parsley, chopped
1	bay leaf
1	tablespoon sea salt or kosher salt
½	teaspoon black pepper
¾	cup Merlot wine
4	pounds mixed fish in season (flounder, bass, whiting, salmon, crab, shrimp, lobster, sole, etc.), cleaned
1	cup water
1	tablespoon tomato paste

In a large saucepan, heat olive oil to medium-hot and sauté garlic and scallions until tender. Add tomatoes or tomato juice, carrot, celery, parsley, bay leaf, salt and pepper. Simmer, uncovered, for 10 minutes, stirring occasionally, then add wine and simmer for 10 minutes more. Add fish, water, and tomato paste; simmer, uncovered, for 15 minutes. Adjust seasonings to taste.

Serves 4 to 6

Serve with Merlot.

Venetian Style White Bean Soup

1	cup white beans, soaked in cold water overnight, drained
1	pound beef stew meat
3½	cups cold water
¼	cup olive oil
2	cloves garlic, minced
2	tablespoons fresh parsley, chopped
$^1/_3$	teaspoon dried rosemary
$^1/_3$	teaspoon dried thyme
1	tablespoon flour
1	tablespoon tomato paste
½	cup Merlot wine
1	teaspoon sea salt or kosher salt
½	teaspoon black pepper
1	cup small dry macaroni

In a large saucepan over medium heat, place drained beans and stew meat in the cold water. Cover and simmer for 1½ hours.

In a heavy skillet, heat olive oil to medium-hot and sauté garlic, parsley, rosemary, and thyme until garlic is tender. Add flour, stirring continuously, until mixture is well blended. Simmer, uncovered, for 6 minutes. Add tomato paste and Merlot wine. Simmer sauce for 10 minutes longer, stirring occasionally.

When beans have cooked 1½ hours, add sauce, salt and pepper. Simmer 2 hours longer, or until beans are tender. Add more water if soup is too thick. Add macaroni, cook for 10 to 12 minutes, stirring occasionally. Adjust salt, pepper, and wine to taste. Remove from stove and let stand 20 minutes before serving.

Serves 6

Serve with Merlot.

Quick and Easy Egg Drop Soup

3 large eggs, separated
4 tablespoons grated Parmesan cheese
 Dash of nutmeg
6 cups beef broth
½ cup Merlot wine
 Croutons for garnish
 Parmesan cheese for garnish

In a deep bowl, beat egg whites until almost stiff. Fold in yolks, cheese and nutmeg. Bring broth and Merlot wine to a boil; stir in egg mixture. Remove from stove immediately.

To serve, pour into individual warm bowls, sprinkle with additional Parmesan cheese and croutons.

Serves 6

Serve with Merlot.

Geer

9

Cauliflower and Broccoli Soup

1	small cauliflower
1	bunch of broccoli florets (tops of 3 to 4 stalks)
¼	cup olive oil
1	medium onion, chopped
¼	cup finely chopped ham
¼	cup finely chopped bacon
1	tablespoon tomato paste
¾	cup Merlot wine
3	quarts beef broth
1	teaspoon sea salt or kosher salt
½	teaspoon black pepper
1	cup small dry macaroni or other small pasta
½	cup grated Parmesan cheese

Remove leaves of cauliflower and cut off any bruised or dirty spots. Place it top downward in a deep bowl of cold salted water for 30 minutes. Drain. Break cauliflower and broccoli florets into bite-sized pieces.

In a large saucepan, heat olive oil to medium-hot and sauté onion, ham and bacon until soft. Add tomato paste and Merlot; simmer for 5 minutes. Add cauliflower and broccoli; simmer for 10 minutes more. Add broth, salt, pepper, and macaroni. Cover and cook for 30 to 45 minutes. Stir in Parmesan cheese.

Sprinkle with additional Parmesan cheese when serving.

Serves 4

Serve with Merlot wine.

Spinach Soup with Basil and Merlot

1	pound fresh spinach, cleaned, or 1 package frozen spinach
1	quart cold water, lightly salted
3	tablespoons butter
1	tablespoon flour
1	quart milk
½	cup heavy cream
¼	cup fresh shredded basil
¼	teaspoon nutmeg
2	tablespoons Merlot wine
2	tablespoons red wine vinegar
½	teaspoon sea salt or kosher salt
¼	teaspoon black pepper
	Croutons for garnish
	Shredded basil for garnish

In a large saucepan, bring salted water to a boil and cook spinach until tender. Drain and purée in a food processor, or press through a sieve. Set aside.

Using the same large saucepan, melt the butter over medium heat, blend in flour, and add milk. Bring to a boil, add spinach, heavy cream, basil, nutmeg, Merlot, wine vinegar, salt and pepper. Bring to a boil again and serve immediately.

Garnish individual servings with croutons and shredded basil.

Serves 6

Serve with Merlot.

Crab Soup Merlot

½   cup (¼ pound or 1 cube) butter
3   cloves garlic, minced
1   medium onion, finely chopped
1   pound crab meat
10 cups milk
½   cup flour
1   tablespoon prepared mustard
1   tablespoon Worcestershire sauce
2   tablespoons Merlot wine
1   teaspoon Kosher salt
½   teaspoon garlic salt
½   teaspoon white pepper
    Dash tabasco sauce
    Paprika for garnish

In a medium saucepan over medium heat, melt butter and sauté garlic and onion until translucent. Add crab meat and continue sautéing for 3 more minutes.

In a large pan, combine milk, flour (mixed with a little of the milk to make a thin paste), mustard, Worcestershire sauce, Merlot, salts, white pepper, and tabasco sauce. Cook over medium heat, stirring continuously until mixture begins to boil. Add crab mixture and return to boil. Adjust seasonings to taste. Serve immediately, garnishing individual servings with paprika. Delicious with sourdough bread.

Serves 8

Serve with Merlot.

Country Corn Chowder

6	slices bacon, chopped
1	large onion, diced
1	clove garlic, minced
6	medium red potatoes, unpeeled, diced
1	10-ounce can chicken broth
2	10-ounce packages frozen corn, preferably small-sized kernels
3	cups milk
2	tablespoons Merlot wine
2	teaspoons granulated sugar
¼	pound butter
2	teaspoons sea salt or kosher salt
¼	teaspoon black pepper
	Crisp bacon for garnish

In a large saucepan over medium heat, cook bacon and remove from pan. In hot bacon grease, sauté onion and garlic until soft. Drain grease from pan and discard.

Add potatoes and chicken broth to pan. Cook 10 minutes. Add remaining ingredients. Add water if thinner soup is desired. Cook over low heat for 10 minutes more. Adjust seasonings to taste.

Serve in warm bowls. Sprinkle crisp, crumbled bacon on top.

Serves 8

Serve with Merlot.

Cold Zuccarrot Soup

1	tablespoon butter
1	onion, finely chopped
½	small bag (8 ounces) baby carrots
1	pound zucchini, thinly sliced
2	10-ounce cans chicken broth
2	tablespoons Merlot wine
1	teaspoon curry powder
¼	cup lemon juice
¼	teaspoon turmeric
1	teaspoon sea salt or kosher salt
	Chives, finely chopped, for garnish

In a large skillet over medium heat, melt butter and sauté onion until it is translucent.

In a food processor or by hand, coarsely chop baby carrots. Add carrots to onion in skillet, cover, and cook for 10 minutes. Add zucchini and cook for 10 minutes more or until tender.

Combine the cooked vegetable mixture with chicken broth, Merlot, curry powder, lemon juice, tumeric and salt. Using half the mixture at a time, purée in a blender or food processor. Adjust salt and add chives to taste.

Chill soup for 2 to 3 hours. Before serving, stir cold soup well, pour into chilled bowls or cups, and sprinkle with chopped chives. Serve immediately.

Serves 6

Serve with Merlot.

Pastas & Grains

Baked Beef and Macaroni Casserole

1½ pounds lean ground beef
1   medium onion, chopped
1   clove garlic, minced
¼   cup olive oil
2   8-ounce cans tomato sauce
4   ripe tomatoes, chopped
1   cup Merlot wine
1½ teaspoons dried oregano
1½ teaspoons dried basil
2   tablespoons chopped fresh parsley
1   tablespoon brown sugar
¼   teaspoon sea salt or kosher salt
¼   teaspoon black pepper
¾   pound dry macaroni
1½ cups grated cheddar cheese (medium-sharp)

Preheat oven to 325° F.

Sauté beef, onion, and garlic in heated olive oil. Add tomato sauce, tomatoes, Merlot wine, herbs, parsley, sugar, salt and pepper. Simmer, uncovered, for 30 minutes, stirring occasionally.

Cook macaroni according to package directions; drain. Add macaroni and ½ cup of the cheese to the sauce. Turn into a 3-quart casserole dish; sprinkle with the remaining cup of cheese. Cover and bake for 45 minutes. Uncover and bake 20 minutes longer.

Serves 6

Serve with Merlot.

Pasta Stuffed Peppers

Peppers never tasted this good . . . substantial enough for a meal or great to do ahead for a barbecue.

2	**large ripe tomatoes**
¼	**cup Merlot wine**
2	**strips pancetta or lean bacon**
2	**small yellow onions, chopped**
2	**cloves garlic, minced**
	Grated rind of 1 lemon
4	**leaves chard, chopped**
¼	**pound orzo or seed pasta**
	Olive oil
1	**teaspoon sea salt or kosher salt**
½	**teaspoon black pepper**
4	**large green, yellow or red bell peppers**

Heat oven to 400° F. Place the whole tomatoes in a pan and bake for 1 hour. Remove tomatoes from pan. On stovetop, deglaze the pan with the Merlot, reserving wine. Chop the tomatoes, reserving the juice, then set aside.

Coarsely chop the pancetta and sauté until crisp, then remove to a paper towel. Sauté the onions, garlic and lemon rind in the same pan. Cook over medium-low heat until the onions are translucent. Add the chard and sauté 5 minutes, scraping the pan to get all the flavorful juices. Add the tomatoes, their juice, and the pancetta to this mixture.

Bring a large pot of water to a rolling boil. Add the pasta and cook until done. Drain and reserve. Place the pasta and the pancetta/tomato mixture into a large bowl. Add a little olive oil, if necessary. Salt and pepper to taste. Toss to combine.

18

Slice off the tops of the peppers, reserving tops. (The tops will be the "lids" once the peppers are stuffed.) Remove the seeds. Fit the peppers snugly into a casserole dish. Spoon the stuffing mixture into the peppers, and replace the lids. Drizzle with olive oil and sprinkle with salt and pepper.

Bake in a 375° F oven for 45 minutes.

Serves 4

Serve with Merlot.

Quick Pesto Pasta Dressing

3	cloves garlic
1	cup fresh basil leaves, tightly packed
1	tablespoon Merlot wine
¼	cup pine nuts, or walnuts or almonds
½	cup grated Parmesan cheese
¼	cup fresh parsley, chopped
½	teaspoon sea salt or kosher salt
¼	teaspoon fresh ground pepper
1	cup olive oil or less

Purée garlic, basil and Merlot in food processor. Add nuts, Parmesan, parsley, salt, pepper and olive oil. Process, scraping sides occasionally. Using a slow, steady stream, pour olive oil into running food processor until dressing is well blended. Adjust salt and pepper to taste. Refrigerate dressing until ready to serve. Use over pasta salad and cold, cooked vegetables.

Yields 1½-2 cups

Serve with Merlot.

19

Zucchini Merlot Linguine

1	tablespoon butter
1	clove garlic, minced
½	cup tomato sauce
½	teaspoon Italian seasoning
½	cup Merlot wine
⅓	cup flour
½	teaspoon sea salt or kosher salt
¼	teaspoon fresh ground pepper
1½	pounds zucchini, sliced crosswise into thin rounds
3	tablespoons olive oil
12	ounces dry linguine, cooked al dente
1	cup Spanish olives, coarsely chopped
½	cup Parmesan or Romano cheese
⅓	cup olive oil

In a heavy skillet over medium heat, melt butter and sauté garlic until soft. Add tomato sauce, Italian seasoning and Merlot. Cover and simmer on low heat for 15 to 20 minutes, stirring occasionally.

In a medium-sized bowl, combine flour, salt, and pepper. Dredge zucchini in seasoned flour mixture until it is lightly coated. Heat 3 tablespoons olive oil in a heavy skillet over medium high heat and sauté small batches of zucchini until golden brown on both sides. Remove each small batch to a plate and keep warm.

Toss cooked pasta, zucchini and chopped olives with ⅓ cup olive oil. Drizzle with garlic-Merlot tomato sauce and sprinkle cheese over all.

Serves 4

Serve with Merlot.

Sausage Pasta Italiano

1	pound Italian-style link sausage
½	cup chopped onion
2	cloves garlic, minced
3½	cups (28-ounce can) tomatoes, undrained
2	cups (15-ounce can) tomato sauce
½	cup Merlot wine
2	tablespoons chopped fresh parsley
2	teaspoons basil
1	teaspoon sugar
½	teaspoon oregano
½	teaspoon sea salt or kosher salt
¼	teaspoon black pepper
2	cups sliced zucchini
3	cups (8 ounces) rotini pasta, uncooked
	Grated Parmesan cheese

In a large skillet, cook sausage until browned on all sides. Remove sausage from pan, slice into thin pieces, then return sausage to pan. Add onion and garlic and sauté until onion is tender but not brown. Drain off excess fat. Add tomatoes with liquid, tomato sauce, Merlot wine, parsley, basil, sugar, oregano, salt and pepper. Bring to a boil. Reduce heat and simmer for 15 minutes, stirring occasionally.

Cook pasta according to package directions and drain. Meanwhile, add zucchini to sausage sauce and simmer 5 to 7 minutes or until crisp-tender. Toss pasta with sauce and serve at once with grated Parmesan cheese.

Serves 4 to 5

Serve with Merlot.

21

Seashell Pasta with Shrimp

1	18-ounce package seashell pasta
1	tablespoon olive oil
4	tablespoons butter
1	clove garlic, minced
1	small onion, chopped
2	tablespoons Worcestershire sauce
¼	cup Merlot wine
½	teaspoon sea salt or kosher salt
¼	teaspoon fresh ground pepper
1½	pounds raw shrimp, peeled and deveined
1	bunch fresh broccoli florets, cut to bite-sized pieces
2	tablespoons Parmesan cheese
2	tablespoons chopped fresh parsley

In a large saucepan, cook pasta according to package directions. Drain pasta and toss with the olive oil. Set aside in a large bowl.

In a heavy skillet, melt butter over medium heat. Sauté garlic and onion until soft. Stir in Worcestershire sauce, Merlot, salt and pepper. Add shrimp and sauté just until pink. Using a slotted spoon, remove shrimp from skillet. Set aside. Simmer wine sauce in skillet until it is reduced to about half. Keep warm.

In a separate saucepan or in the microwave, steam broccoli until crisp-tender; drain. Add broccoli, shrimp and wine sauce to pasta; toss gently. Sprinkle with Parmesan cheese and parsley.

Serves 6

Serve with Merlot.

Spinach and Ham Lasagna

In this dish, noodles need not be cooked before baking.

1	medium onion, finely chopped
1	clove garlic, minced
1	green bell pepper, finely chopped
¼	cup olive oil
4	cups tomato sauce
½	cup Merlot wine
1	teaspoon ground oregano
¾	cup each chopped fresh parsley and basil
1	pound lasagna noodles, uncooked
1½	pounds whole milk ricotta mixed with 1 egg yolk and 1 teaspoon nutmeg
1½	pounds mozzarella cheese, grated
¾	cup grated Parmesan cheese
1	pound ham, thinly sliced and cut into bite-sized pieces
1	pound fresh spinach leaves, washed, steamed for 1 minute and drained

Preheat oven to 350° F. In a large skillet, sauté onion, garlic, and bell pepper in olive oil until tender. Stir in tomato sauce, Merlot wine, and oregano. Simmer, covered, for 10 minutes.

Layer tomato sauce mixture, parsley, basil, pasta, cheeses, ham and spinach in a lasagna pan. Top with grated mozzarella or Parmesan cheese. Cover tightly with aluminum foil and bake 1½ hours, or until pasta is tender. Remove foil during last 30 minutes of cooking to brown top. Cool slightly before cutting.

Serves 12

Serve with Merlot.

Rice with Chicken Livers and Merlot

SAUCE

4	tablespoons butter
4	tablespoons beef broth
2	tablespoons finely chopped onion
8	chicken livers, diced
1	slice lemon peel, about 2 inches long and 1 inch wide
¼	cup Merlot wine
1	teaspoon sea salt or kosher salt
¼	teaspoon fresh ground pepper
½	cup grated Parmesan cheese

RICE

4	tablespoons butter
2	tablespoons finely chopped onion
2	cups rice
6	cups beef broth

Sauce: In a small saucepan over medium heat, add butter, beef broth, and 2 tablespoons onion; simmer for 5 minutes. Add chicken livers and lemon peel; simmer 3 minutes more. Add Merlot, salt and pepper; simmer 10 minutes more. Remove lemon peel.

Rice: While sauce is cooking, melt butter in a large saucepan and sauté 2 tablespoons onion until soft. Add rice, stir, cover, and simmer for 2 or 3 minutes. Add one cup of broth and continue adding a cup of broth at a time, as necessary, until rice is cooked. Adjust seasonings to taste.

Add sauce and one half of the Parmesan cheese to rice. Place in serving dish, sprinkle with remaining cheese, and dot with butter.

Serves 4 to 6

Serve with Merlot.

24

Pasta with Fresh Herb Sauce

1½ cups heavy cream or half and half
¼   cup Merlot wine
¼   cup butter
1   teaspoon sea salt or kosher salt
¼   teaspoon fresh ground pepper
¼   cup grated Romano cheese
1   cup finely chopped mixed fresh herbs — combine
       basil, chives, cilantro, parsley, rosemary, or other
       favorites
1   pound of your favorite pasta, cooked
       Chopped tomato
       Freshly grated Parmesan cheese

In a medium-sized saucepan over medium heat, combine the heavy cream or half and half, Merlot, butter, salt, and pepper. Simmer for 15 minutes, or until sauce is slightly reduced and thickened.

Whisk in Romano cheese and herbs; simmer 5 minutes longer. Adjust seasonings to taste.

Serve immediately over your favorite pasta.

Serves 6

Serve with Merlot.

Tamale Pie with Cornbread Crust

1   large onion, chopped
2   tablespoons cooking oil
1½ pounds ground round or other lean ground meat
1   cup tomato sauce
¾   cup Merlot wine
1   12-ounce can whole-kernel corn
½   cup chopped green bell pepper
½   cup chopped red bell pepper
2   4¼-ounce cans chopped ripe olives
2   tablespoon chili powder
½   teaspoon cumin powder
½   cup fresh chopped cilantro
1   teaspoon sea salt or kosher salt
     Sour cream for garnish
     Fresh chopped cilantro for garnish

CORNBREAD
½   cup all-purpose flour
¾   cup yellow cornmeal
2   teaspoons granulated sugar
1   teaspoon baking powder
½   teaspoon baking soda
1   teaspoon salt
1   cup buttermilk
2   tablespoons cooking oil

Preheat oven to 400° F. In a large skillet over medium heat, sauté onion in oil until tender. Add meat and sauté until browned, stirring to break apart. Skim excess grease from pan and discard.

Add remaining ingredients to meat mixture, stir well, and simmer for 5 minutes. Adjust seasonings to taste. Pour mixture into an 8 x 12-inch baking dish and cover with cornbread batter.

Cornbread: Mix and sift dry ingredients. In a separate bowl, combine egg and buttermilk; add to dry ingredients with a few, quick strokes, stirring just until mixed. Stir in oil with a few, quick strokes. Spread batter evenly over meat mixture and bake, uncovered, for 30 minutes or until cornbread is golden brown.

To serve, top with dollops of sour cream sprinkled with parsley.

Serve with Merlot.   Serves 8

Armenian Pilaf

¼   **cup butter**
1   **clove garlic, minced**
½   **cup chopped fresh parsley**
1½   **cups uncooked rice**
3   **cups beef broth**
1   **cup Merlot wine**
1   **teaspoon sea salt or kosher salt**
½   **teaspoon black pepper**

In a heavy skillet, melt butter and sauté garlic until soft. Add rice and cook, stirring frequently, until butter begins to bubble. Add remaining ingredients, cover, and simmer for 30 minutes. Remove cover, stir rice gently, and bake 10 minutes more.

                                                 Serves 6

Serve with Merlot.

Marvelous Merlot Macaroni

1   8-ounce package shell or elbow macaroni, cooked
2   tablespoons olive oil
1   small onion, finely chopped
2   cloves garlic, minced
½   pound lean ground beef
½   pound cheddar cheese, grated
1½   cups tomato sauce
½   cup Merlot wine
6   fresh mushrooms, sliced
1   small bottle pimiento-stuffed olives
     Salt and pepper to taste

Preheat oven to 350° F.

In a large saucepan over high heat, cook pasta according to package directions; drain and set aside.

In a heavy skillet over medium heat, heat oil and sauté onion and garlic until soft. Add ground beef and cook, stirring to break apart, until meat is well-browned. Add remaining ingredients; stir to mix. Combine with cooked macaroni, pour into a greased 8 x 12-inch casserole, cover and bake for ½ hour. Remove cover and bake for ½ longer.

Serves 6

Serve with Merlot.

Beppa's Black Beans and Rice Merlot

1½ cups dry black beans
1 small onion, halved
1 bay leaf
4 cups water
3 tablespoons olive oil
4 cloves garlic, minced
2 cups chopped onions
2 4-ounce cans chopped mild green chiles
2 teaspoons powdered cumin
1 tablespoon chili powder
2 teaspoons lemon juice
½ cup Merlot wine
1 teaspoon sea salt or kosher salt
½ teaspoon black pepper
2 tablespoons chopped fresh cilantro
2 tablespoons sour cream

Rinse and soak beans in a large, heavy pan filled with cool water for 6 to 8 hours or overnight. Drain, rinse, and drain again. Return beans to pan. Add halved onion, bay leaf and 4 cups of water. Bring to a boil, reduce heat, cover, and simmer for approximately 1½ hours or until beans are tender. Remove and discard onion and bay leaf.

Heat oil in a large skillet over medium heat. Sauté garlic and onion until soft. Add green chiles, cumin, chili powder, lemon juice, Merlot wine, salt, pepper, and cilantro; cook and stir for 2 minutes. Add the onion mixture to the bean pan. Bring to a boil, reduce heat, and simmer, uncovered, for 5 to 10 minutes or until liquids thicken slightly. Garnish with sour cream and cilantro sprigs.

Serves 4 to 6

Serve with Merlot.

Quick Pasta with Shrimp, Feta and Merlot

2	**tablespoons olive oil**
¼	**cup Merlot wine**
1	**clove garlic, minced**
1	**cup small cooked shrimp**
1	**pound feta cheese, crumbled**
6	**green onions, finely chopped**
1	**cup fresh basil**
4	**fresh tomatoes, finely chopped**
½	**teaspoon sea salt or kosher salt**
¼	**teaspoon white pepper**
1	**16-ounce package any pasta**

In a large bowl, combine olive oil, Merlot, garlic, shrimp, feta cheese, green onions, basil, tomatoes, salt and pepper. Stir well to combine, adjust seasonings to taste, and let stand at room temperature for at least 1 hour.

Prepare pasta according to package directions; drain well.

Add hot pasta to sauce and toss. Serve immediately.

Serves 4

Serve with Merlot.

Geer

Meats

Merlot and Chocolate Ragout

The unusual combination of ingredients in this ragout is delicious and memorable.

1	**pound beef stew meat**
1	**pound lamb stew meat**
1	**pound pork stew meat**
2	**cups Merlot wine**
3	**tablespoons fresh chopped sage**
2	**teaspoons ground cumin**
½	**teaspoon chili powder**
½	**teaspoon ground pepper**
4	**tablespoons butter**
3	**cloves garlic, minced**
1	**cup beef stock**
1	**teaspoon sea salt or kosher salt**
2	**ounces bittersweet chocolate, chopped**
1	**sweet potato, steamed or blanched**
2	**turnips, steamed or blanched**
3	**carrots, steamed or blanched**

Marinate the meats overnight in the Merlot, sage, cumin, chili powder and pepper. Lift meat from marinade and dry with paper towels. Bring the marinade to a boil and strain. Discard any solids.

Melt butter in a large skillet and add the meat. Cook until well-browned. Add the garlic and cook 1 minute more. Add the marinade, stock and salt. Simmer about 1 hour or until meat seems tender but is not falling apart. Add the chocolate and let melt completely. Add the cooked vegetables and simmer about 15 minutes. Correct seasonings with salt and pepper. Serve over rice.

Serves 8

Serve with Merlot.

Rabbit Cacciatore Lombard Style

1	tablespoon olive oil
2	rabbit breasts, cut in two
4	rabbit thighs
½	medium onion, chopped finely
1	carrot, chopped finely
1	celery stalk, chopped finely
2	large sprigs fresh rosemary
16	ounces chicken stock
8	ounces mushrooms, chopped
6	ounces Merlot wine
	Salt and pepper to taste
	Arrowroot or cornstarch for thickening, if desired

In a large, heavy skillet or cast iron Dutch oven over medium-hot heat, brown rabbit pieces in the olive oil. Add the finely chopped onion, carrot, and celery, and sauté until the onions are translucent. Add the rosemary and chicken stock to almost cover the rabbit pieces and simmer for 30 minutes, or until the rabbit is cooked through.

Add the mushrooms and simmer for another 10 minutes. Add the Merlot wine and continue to simmer for another 5 minutes. Salt and pepper to taste. If desired, stir in the arrowroot or cornstarch to thicken slightly.

Serves 4

Serve with Merlot wine.

Blue Cheese Tenderloin with Merlot Sauce

½   cup butter
½   cup Merlot wine
3   pounds pork tenderloin
1   teaspoon sea salt or kosher salt
½   tablespoon fresh ground black pepper
1   tablespoon flour
6   ounces fresh blue cheese
¾   cup whipping cream
½   pint fresh raspberries

Preheat oven to 350° F.

Pat entire tenderloin(s) with black pepper and sprinkle with salt.

In a large skillet over medium heat, melt ¼ cup butter and stir in Merlot. Braise seasoned tenderloin until it is golden brown. Transfer tenderloin to an 8 x 12-inch glass baking dish.

Add remaining butter, flour and whipping cream to the seasoned pan, using a whisk to blend until smooth and creamy. Pour mixture over tenderloin and crumble blue cheese over the top of the roast.

Bake for 45 minutes. Garnish with raspberries.

Serves 6

Serve with Merlot wine.

35

London Broil Merlot

2	London broil or top round roasts (1½ pounds each), 2½ to 3½ inches thick
3	cloves garlic, minced
1	small onion, minced
¼	cup soy sauce
¼	cup brown sugar
1	cup Merlot wine
¼	cup lemon juice
3	tablespoons Worcestershire sauce
2	tablespoons olive oil
½	cup tomato ketchup or tomato paste
1	teaspoon sea salt or kosher salt
½	teaspoon freshly ground black pepper
1	cup water

Place the meat in a single layer in a nonreactive baking dish. Combine all remaining ingredients and pour over the meat. Cover and refrigerate for at least six hours or overnight. Turn and baste meat several times while it is marinating.

Preheat the grill.

Remove the marinated meat from the refrigerator an hour before grilling. Grill it for 6 to 7 minutes per side, turning and basting several times, until cooked to preference. To ensure juiciness, do not pierce the meat with a fork during grilling. To serve, cut meat into ¼-inch slices diagonally against the grain.

Serves 8

Serve with Merlot.

Beef Stew with Merlot

5	medium onions, sliced thin
2	tablespoons bacon drippings or cooking oil
3	pounds lean beef stew meat, cut in 1-inch cubes
2	tablespoons flour
1	teaspoon sea salt or kosher salt
½	teaspoon black pepper
1	teaspoon thyme
1	teaspoon marjoram
2	cups beef broth
1	cup Merlot wine
1	cup peeled baby carrots
½	pound fresh mushrooms, sliced

In a large, heavy skillet over medium heat, sauté onions in bacon drippings until brown; remove from pan and set aside. Add meat and brown it in the same pan. When browned, sprinkle meat with a mixture of the flour, salt, pepper, thyme and marjoram.

Add broth and Merlot, mixing well. Stir in cooked onions. Reduce heat and simmer, covered, for 3 hours. Add additional broth and Merlot as needed to keep meat barely covered. Continue simmering until meat is tender.

During the last half-hour of cooking add the carrots and mushrooms.

Serves 8

Serve with Merlot.

37

Stuffed Roast Pork

6	dried prunes, coarsely chopped
6	dried apricots, coarsely chopped
½	cup golden raisins
6	toasted pecans, chopped
3	cloves garlic, chopped
1	cup Merlot wine
2	pork tenderloins (approximately 1 to 1½ pounds each)
	Salt and pepper
6	apples
6	medium onions, peeled

Combine the prunes, apricots, raisins, pecans, and garlic in a small bowl. Add the Merlot and set aside to soak. Preheat oven to 350° F.

Make a lengthwise cut in the pork tenderloins, but do not cut all the way through. Flatten slightly with the side of a cleaver or a rolling pin. Spread the fruit and nut mixture over the tenderloins and season with salt and pepper. Roll the roasts and tie with string. Season the outside liberally with salt and pepper.

Surround the tenderloins with the apples and onions. Roast, allowing 30 minutes per pound. (If you do not want the apples and onions to simmer in the pork's fatty juices, place them in a separate pan and roast in the oven with the tenderloin.)

To serve, slice the pork tenderloins into 1-inch thick slices. Place on plates with the pan-roasted apples and onions.

Serves 4 to 6

Serve with Merlot.

Grilled Butterflied Leg of Lamb

1   leg of lamb (5 pounds), butterflied
(Ask your butcher to butterfly the leg of lamb.)

MARINADE:
1   cup olive oil
¼   cup soy sauce or Worcestershire sauce
1   cup chopped fresh mint
½   cup coarsely chopped fresh rosemary
4   cloves garlic, minced
1   cup Merlot wine
Salt and pepper

Combine the marinade ingredients in a nonreactive roasting pan and place the lamb fat-side up in the liquid. Marinate for 6 hours or overnight, turning several times.

Grill over a medium-hot fire, turning several times, until tender and slightly pink inside.

Serves 6 to 8

Serve with Merlot.

39

Savory Herbed Rack of Lamb

MARINADE

½	cup Merlot wine
¼	cup balsamic vinegar
¼	cup soy sauce
2	heaping tablespoons Dijon mustard
2	heaping teaspoons minced fresh garlic
½	teaspoon rosemary
½	teaspoon oregano
½	teaspoon marjoram
½	teaspoon thyme
1	teaspoon oregano
2	tablespoons olive oil
2	racks of lamb, trimmed of all fat and silverskin
1	tablespoon cooking oil

Combine all marinade ingredients in a large glass or nonreactive baking dish. Mix well. Add lamb and marinate at least 2 hours or overnight.

Preheat oven to 450° F. Over high heat, heat cooking oil in a heavy sauté pan. Remove racks of lamb from marinade; discard marinade. Sear meat in hot oil on all sides until nicely browned. Bake in 450° F oven 8 to 12 minutes for medium rare. Remove from oven and let rest for 2 to 4 minutes.

Slice lamb into chops and serve.

Serves 8

Serve with Merlot.

Roast Pork Tenderloin with Lavender and Mint

½	cup finely chopped fresh mint
2	tablespoons coarsely chopped dried lavender
2	teaspoons finely minced fresh garlic
4	tablespoons soy sauce
2	tablespoons freshly squeezed orange juice
2	tablespoons olive oil
⅓	cup Merlot wine
2	pork tenderloins (10 ounces each), trimmed of all fat and silverskin
½	teaspoon sea salt or kosher salt
½	teaspoon black pepper
2	tablespoons cooking oil

Mix mint, lavender, garlic, soy sauce, orange juice, olive oil and Merlot. Add pork, coating all sides. Cover and marinate in refrigerator overnight. Remove pork from marinade. Wipe off most of the herbs and spices. Discard marinade.

Preheat oven to 425° F. Season each pork tenderloin with salt and pepper. Then, in a large skillet that has been lightly coated with cooking oil, over medium-high heat, sear meat on all sides.

Place pork in a baking pan and roast in oven for 20 to 30 minutes or until meat is cooked through. Remove meat from oven; let it rest, loosely covered, for 3 to 4 minutes. Slice thinly and serve.

Serves 6 to 8

Serve with Merlot.

Merlot Meat Loaf

1	cup coarse bread crumbs
¾	cup Merlot wine
2	pounds ground beef
1	pound ground pork
1	large onion, finely chopped
4	cloves garlic, minced
1	cup chopped stuffed green olives
½	cup tomato paste
2	teaspoons grainy French mustard
2	teaspoons chopped fresh basil
2	teaspoons chopped parsley
½	teaspoon sea salt or Kosher salt
½	teaspoon black pepper
3	eggs, beaten

Preheat oven to 350° F. Combine bread crumbs and wine in a small bowl. Set aside.

In a mixing bowl, thoroughly combine the beef, pork, onion, garlic, olives, tomato paste, mustard, basil, parsley, salt and pepper. Beat the eggs slightly, then add eggs and soaked bread crumbs to the meat mixture.

Form into a 4-inch thick loaf, and place in the center of a good-sized roasting pan so the meat is not touching the sides.

Bake for 1½ hours, basting several times with pan juices and additional wine, to form a crispy crust. Serve hot or at room temperature.

Serves 6 to 8

Serve with Merlot.

Shallot and Rosemary Glazed Steak

4	4- to 6-ounce top sirloin steaks, 1 to 2 inches thick
1	teaspoon sea salt or kosher salt
½	teaspoon fresh ground pepper
⅓	cup olive oil
⅔	cup Merlot wine
3	3-inch fresh rosemary sprigs, chopped
3	cloves garlic, peeled and slightly mashed
4	tablespoons olive oil
2	tablespoons minced shallots
1	tablespoon butter

Season steaks with salt and pepper and place in a shallow container. Add ⅓ cup olive oil, ⅓ cup Merlot, rosemary and garlic. Marinate for several hours or overnight.

Heat 2 to 3 tablespoons olive oil in heavy skillet and cook steaks until brown and crusty (1 to 2 minutes per side). Remove steaks.

Add to the hot skillet: 1 tablespoon olive oil and shallots and sauté until tender. Add remaining ⅓ cup Merlot and cook over medium high heat, scraping all of the brown crusty pieces from the pan. Cook glaze until liquid is reduced by half; stir in butter. Slice each steak and drizzle with glaze before serving.

Serves 4

Serve with Merlot.

43

Lamb Stew Merlot

2	pounds lamb stew meat, trimmed of fat
3	tablespoons olive oil
1	medium onion, diced
3	medium carrots, diced
2	cloves garlic, minced
2	slices unpeeled orange
1	long strip of lemon peel
1	cup Merlot wine
1	cup tomato juice
1	teaspoon ground cloves
1	stick cinnamon
1	teaspoon powdered coriander
2	tablespoons flour
	Salt and pepper

Preheat oven to 325° F. In a medium Dutch oven, brown lamb lightly in hot olive oil. Add onion, carrots and garlic; sauté briefly. Add the orange, lemon peel, Merlot wine, tomato juice, ground cloves, cinnamon and coriander. Cover and bring to a simmer on top of stove. Place in preheated oven. Bake until tender, about 1½ to 2 hours. Check occasionally. If more liquid is needed, add additional equal amounts of wine and tomato juice.

When lamb is tender, remove excess grease, cinnamon stick, orange slices and lemon peel. Thicken sauce with the flour to which you have added a small amount of water to make a paste. Season with salt and pepper. More wine may be added if there is not enough sauce.

Serves 4-6

Serve with Merlot.

Sauerbraten

This is a classic German recipe.

2	teaspoons sea salt or kosher salt
½	teaspoon freshly ground pepper
4	pounds beef round or chuck, suitable for pot roast
½	cup finely sliced onion
½	cup red wine vinegar
1½	cups Merlot wine
½	cup cold water
2	tablespoons butter, melted
12	gingersnap cookies, crumbled
1	teaspoon sugar
1	cup hot water

Rub salt and pepper into beef, and place in roasting pan with onion, vinegar, ½ cup of the Merlot wine, and the cold water. Cover the pan and roast in oven at 350° F for 4 hours, basting frequently.

When meat is done, make the gravy. Mix together the butter, gingersnaps and sugar. Add hot water and the remaining Merlot. Cook for 5 minutes or until thickened. Strain the wine and cooking juices from the roast and add to the gravy. Stir until smooth.

To serve, place slices on platter or plates. Pour gravy over, or serve the gravy separately in a gravy boat.

Serves 6

Serve with Merlot.

Savory Swiss Steak

2	pounds beef round steak
¼	cup flour
2	tablespoons shortening
1	clove garlic, minced
1	teaspoon sea salt or kosher salt
½	teaspoon black pepper
½	teaspoon fresh ground ginger
½	teaspoon marjoram
¼	cup Merlot wine
1	large onion, chopped
3	large tomatoes, chopped
1	10½-ounce can beef broth
¼	cup water

Preheat oven to 325° F. For more tender meat, pound the steak with a meat mallet. Dredge both sides of meat with flour. In large skillet, heat shortening to medium-high heat. Add meat and brown well on both sides. Transfer to a baking dish.

Blend together the garlic, salt, pepper, ginger, marjoram, Merlot wine, onion and tomatoes. Spread evenly over steak. Gently pour beef broth and water over meat.

Cover and bake the steak for 2 to 2½ hours, basting several times with pan drippings while baking.

Serves 6

Serve with Merlot.

46

Poultry

Merlot Casserole Chicken

4	pounds young chicken, cut up
	Salt and pepper to taste
	Pinch of thyme
	Pinch of marjoram
4	tablespoons olive oil
3	tablespoons butter
½	pound raw, lean ham slices, cut into thin strips
3	carrots, scraped and sliced
2	medium onions, thinly sliced
1	cup Merlot wine
½	cup chicken stock
1	clove garlic, mashed
1	teaspoon cloves
1	teaspoon tarragon
1	bay leaf

Wash and pat chicken pieces dry, then season them with a mixture of salt, pepper, thyme and marjoram. Heat olive oil until it is very hot in a casserole, add the chicken pieces and brown evenly, turning frequently. Drain off the olive oil.

In a separate bowl, combine the butter mixed with the ham, carrots, onions, Merlot wine, chicken stock, garlic and herbs. Mix thoroughly and add to the chicken in the casserole dish.

Cover and cook over low flame for 45 minutes, until chicken is well cooked.

Serves 6 to 8

Serve with Merlot.

49

Glazed Cornish Hens with Merlot Sauce

4   game hens

GLAZE
2   tablespoons butter
½   cup raspberry jelly
2   tablespoons lemon juice
¼   cup Merlot wine

STUFFING
2½   cups chicken broth
½   cup wild rice
2   tablespoons butter
½   cup brown rice
1   medium onion, diced
8   ounces fresh mushrooms, sliced
¼   cup chopped celery
½   cup chopped pecans
2   tablespoons chopped fresh parsley
¼   teaspoon thyme
1   teaspoon sea salt or Kosher salt
½   teaspoon ground pepper

Bring glaze ingredients to a boil and reduce. Set aside.

Wash game hens and pat dry. In a medium saucepan, bring the chicken broth to a boil. Add wild rice and 1 tablespoon butter. Cover and cook over low heat for 12 to 14 minutes. Add brown rice, cover, and continue cooking for 45 minutes or until all liquid is absorbed. Add remaining tablespoon butter and fluff with a fork.

Sauté onion, mushrooms and celery in 2 tablespoons butter until onions are transparent and celery is limp. Add to the cooked rice along with pecans, parsley, thyme, salt and pepper.

Preheat oven to 350° F.

Stuff hens with rice mixture. Put extra stuffing mixture in a greased casserole and place in oven with game hens during the last 45 minutes of baking. Bake hens for 1½ hours, basting frequently with glaze. When done, remove hens from pan and pour off grease, reserving pan juices for gravy. Stir cornstarch and water mixture into pan juices to thicken gravy.

Serves 4

Serve with Merlot.

Oriental Chicken

½	**cup soy sauce**
½	**cup Merlot wine**
½	**cup pineapple juice**
1	**teaspoon curry powder**
1	**teaspoon Dijon mustard**
1	**clove garlic, minced**
1	**frying chicken, cut into serving pieces**

In a large bowl, combine soy sauce, Merlot, pineapple juice, curry, mustard and garlic; mix well. Add chicken and coat thoroughly with marinade. Cover and refrigerate for at least 4 hours or overnight.

Barbecue chicken or bake in a 350° F oven for 1 hour.

Serves 4

Serve with Merlot.

Broccoli Chicken with Merlot Plum Sauce

2	tablespoons olive oil
4	skinless, boneless chicken breasts, cut into thin strips
4	cups broccoli florets
1	cup chicken broth, warm
¼	cup sliced green onion
½	cup diagonally sliced celery
¼	pound mushrooms, sliced
1	8-ounce can water chestnuts, sliced
¼	teaspoon black pepper
2	tablespoons cornstarch
¼	cup soy sauce
½	cup red plum jam
2	tablespoons Merlot wine
3	tablespoons sesame seeds, toasted

In large frying pan, heat olive oil until hot and stir-fry chicken strips about 2 minutes. Add broccoli, stirring and cooking 2 minutes more. Add 2 tablespoons chicken broth and stir in onion and celery, cooking 2 minutes. Add mushrooms and 2 tablespoons more chicken broth, cooking 2 minutes. Add water chestnuts and pepper, stirring and cooking 1 minute.

In a small bowl, stir together cornstarch and soy sauce until smooth. Add remaining 3/4 cup broth to chicken and vegetables, pushing them to side of pan. Slowly stir soy mixture into broth until it thickens, then stir everything in pan together.

In a small saucepan, mix plum jam with Merlot and heat until jam melts. Place chicken mixture in shallow serving bowl and drizzle Merlot-plum sauce over all. Sprinkle with sesame seeds.

Serves 4

Serve with Merlot.

Turkey Cacciatore

½   **cup thinly sliced onion**
½   **cup finely chopped bell pepper**
2   **tablespoons butter**
1   **cup sliced mushrooms**
2   **cloves garlic, minced**
1   **8-ounce can stewed tomatoes**
1   **8-ounce can tomato sauce**
¼   **cup Merlot wine**
1   **bay leaf**
2   **teaspoons granulated sugar**
½   **teaspoon dried basil**
½   **teaspoon dried thyme**
½   **teaspoon dried oregano**
½   **teaspoon sea salt or kosher salt**
4   **turkey thighs**

In a 3-quart saucepan over medium heat, sauté onion and bell pepper in butter until onion is transparent and pepper is crisp-tender. Add mushrooms and garlic; cook for 2 to 3 minutes.

Stir in tomatoes, tomato sauce, Merlot wine, bay leaf, sugar, basil, thyme, oregano and salt. Bring to a boil. Add turkey thighs. Reduce heat to low; cover and cook for 1 to 1½ hours or until turkey is tender and easily pulls away from bone.

Delicious over hot pasta.

Serves 4 to 6

Serve with Merlot.

Turkey Layer-Bake with Spaghetti Squash

1   spaghetti squash, approximately 4 pounds
8   tablespoons olive oil
3   medium zucchini, sliced ¼-inch thick
1   pound button mushrooms, halved
1   large red onion, halved and sliced thin
3   cloves garlic, minced
       Flour for dusting
2   pounds turkey breast slices, ⅓-inch thick
¾   cup Merlot wine
1   28-ounce can crushed tomatoes
⅓   cup minced fresh basil
½   cup plus 3 tablespoons minced fresh parsley
1   cup grated Parmesan or Romano cheese
2   tablespoons fresh chopped chives

Cut spaghetti squash in half lengthwise; remove seeds. Place both halves cut side down on a baking sheet and bake at 350° F for 40 minutes. Cool. Remove "spaghetti" from squash halves and put into bottom of lightly oiled 9 x 13-inch glass baking dish.

In a sauté pan, heat 3 tablespoons of the olive oil to medium hot and sauté the zucchini, mushrooms, and onions for 5 minutes. Add the garlic and cook for 2 minutes more. Remove vegetables from pan and place on top of the spaghetti squash, leaving a center strip open for the turkey. In the same sauté pan, heat 3 tablespoons of the olive oil. Sauté flour-dusted turkey slices for 2 minutes per side. Remove from pan and layer down center of baking dish. Add Merlot wine to deglaze the sauté pan, then pour over turkey.

Put the same pan back on the heat. Add the remaining 2 tablespoons olive oil, tomatoes, basil and parsley. Simmer on medium heat for 6 minutes, then drizzle over the vegetables in the baking dish. Sprinkle cheese over the entire dish and cover with foil.

At this point, this one-dish dinner can be refrigerated overnight or cooked at once. When ready to cook, bake, covered, on the middle rack of a 350º F oven for 30 minutes. Then remove the foil for 10 minutes. Garnish with parsley and chives.

Serve with green salad and French bread.   Serves 6 to 8

Serve with Merlot.

Spicy Chili Chicken

2	tablespoons olive oil
6	chicken breast halves, boned and skinned, cubed
1	medium onion, finely chopped
1	green bell pepper, finely chopped
½	cup Merlot wine
2	cloves garlic, minced
1	15½-ounce can Mexican-style stewed tomatoes
2	teaspoons chili powder
1	teaspoon ground cumin
½	teaspoon sea salt or kosher salt

In a large skillet over medium heat, sauté chicken, onion, pepper and garlic in olive oil until chicken is no longer pink inside. Add remaining ingredients and simmer 20 minutes. Serve over steamed rice.

Serves 4 to 6

Serve with Merlot.

Chicken Braised in Red Wine Sauce (Coq au Vin)

2   **tablespoons butter**
1   **chicken, cut up**
1   **clove garlic, minced**
10   **ounces pearl onions, peeled**
4   **slices bacon, cut into 1-inch pieces**
1   **tablespoon flour**
¾   **cup chicken broth**
2   **tablespoon Merlot wine**
½   **teaspoon dried thyme**
½   **teaspoon dried basil**
       Salt and black pepper to taste

In a large skillet over medium-high heat, melt the butter and sauté the chicken until it is golden brown; place it in a heavy casserole. In same skillet, sauté garlic, onions, and bacon; spoon them into the casserole.

Remove all but 2 tablespoons fat from the skillet. Add the flour and stir well. Add chicken broth, 1 tablespoon of the Merlot wine, herbs, salt and pepper. Stir and pour over chicken. Cover and simmer for 30 minutes. Remove from heat and stir in the other tablespoon of Merlot.

Remove any excess grease from sauce before serving.

Serves 4

Serve with Merlot.

Chicken and Shrimp in Merlot Sauce

3   pound chicken, cut up
1   tablespoon sea salt or kosher salt
¼   teaspoon black pepper
¼   cup flour
½   cup olive oil

SAUCE
1   large onion, finely chopped
2   cloves garlic, minced
3   tablespoons chopped fresh parsley
1   cup Merlot wine
1½   teaspoons dried Italian seasoning
½   cup tomato sauce
1   teaspoon dried basil
1   pound large shrimp, shelled and deveined

Wash chicken and pat dry. In a plastic bag, combine salt, pepper and flour. Add chicken to bag, a few pieces at a time, and shake to coat thoroughly with seasoned flour.

In a large skillet, heat oil to medium hot. Add chicken pieces and sauté until golden brown. Remove chicken and set aside.

Add onions and garlic to skillet and sauté until soft. Add parsley, Merlot, Italian seasoning, tomato sauce and basil; stir to combine. Return chicken to skillet, cover and cook for 30 minutes or until chicken is tender. Place chicken on serving platter and keep warm.

Add shrimp to Merlot sauce and cook, uncovered, until sauce bubbles and shrimp just turn pink. Skim any fat from surface of sauce. Pour shrimp sauce over chicken. Serve.

Serves 4 to 6

Serve with Merlot.

57

Roast Wild Duck

2	ducks, cut in half
2	cloves garlic, minced
1	large onion, chopped
1	cup finely chopped celery
1	cup bottled chili sauce
1	tablespoon Worcestershire sauce
1	tablespoon dry mustard
½	tablespoon nutmeg
	Juice of 1 lemon
½	cup Merlot wine
2	cups water
	Paprika

Preheat oven to 325° F. Wash and pat ducks dry. Rub duck halves with garlic, salt and pepper. Place breast-side down in roasting pan.

In heavy skillet, sauté onion, garlic and celery for 5 minutes. Add remaining ingredients except paprika, bring to a boil, then reduce heat and simmer for 5 minutes. Pour over ducks. Bake, covered, for 3 hours. When ducks are tender, turn breast-side up and sprinkle with paprika. Bake uncovered until brown. Serve with gravy in pan.

To thicken gravy, make a paste of two to three tablespoons flour and a little water. Add a small amount of hot drippings to mixture and stir, then gradually stir into gravy in pan. Continue stirring and cook until thickened.

Serves 4

Serve with Merlot.

Sweet and Sour Chicken

4   chicken breast halves, boned and skinned
2   tablespoons flour
1   teaspoon sea salt or kosher salt
½   teaspoon black pepper
2   tablespoons olive oil

SAUCE
½   cup bottled chili sauce
½   cup ketchup
½   cup Merlot wine
½   cup honey
2   tablespoons lemon juice
2½ teaspoons cornstarch
1   teaspoon garlic salt
½   cup chopped cashews for garnish

Wash chicken breasts and pat dry. In a bowl or plastic bag, mix flour, salt and pepper; dredge chicken breasts with flour mixture.

Heat olive oil in a large skillet over medium-high heat; sauté the chicken breasts for 6 to 8 minutes, turning occasionally, until chicken is lightly browned and juices run clear when meat is pierced with a fork. Transfer chicken to a serving platter and keep warm.

To make sauce, combine chili sauce, ketchup, Merlot, honey, lemon juice, cornstarch and garlic salt. Cook and stir over medium heat for 2 to 3 minutes, or until mixture boils and thickens. Spoon over chicken. Garnish with chopped cashews.

Serves 4

Serve with Merlot.

Spanish Chicken in Casserole

¼   cup olive oil
2   cloves garlic, minced
1   medium onion, finely chopped
4   pounds chicken parts — breasts, thighs, legs
1   cup Merlot wine
2   large tomatoes, chopped
4   green onions, chopped
1   green bell pepper, finely chopped
2   whole cloves
1   bay leaf
1   teaspoon oregano
2   teaspoons sea salt or kosher salt
½   teaspoon black pepper
1½ cup any rice, uncooked
1   cup coarsely chopped ripe olives
¼   cup snipped sun-dried tomatoes

Preheat oven to 350° F.

Heat olive oil in a large skillet over medium-high heat; sauté garlic and onion until soft. Add chicken and brown lightly. Add Merlot, tomatoes, green onion, green pepper, and seasonings; simmer for 5 minutes. Pour into a large casserole.

In the same skillet, add uncooked rice and sauté, stirring continuously, until golden; add to chicken in casserole. Cover with water and bake for 1 ½ hours or until chicken is tender. Stir in olives and sun-dried tomatoes. Adjust seasonings and add more Merlot if desired.

Serves 6

Serve with Merlot.

Seafood

Deviled Crab Casserole

3	tablespoons butter
3	tablespoons flour
2	cups heavy cream
1	small jar chopped pimientos, drained
2	tablespoons finely chopped green bell pepper
1	tablespoon chopped parsley
¼	cup Merlot wine
1	teaspoon Worcestershire sauce
¼	cup lemon juice
½	teaspoon dry mustard
1	teaspoon sea salt or kosher salt
½	teaspoon cayenne pepper
2	cups flaked fresh or canned crabmeat
2	hard-boiled eggs, chopped
½	cup grated Parmesan cheese
½	cup grated medium-sharp cheddar cheese

Preheat oven to 375° F.

In a large saucepan over medium heat, melt butter, stir in flour, and cook, stirring continuously, for 1 to 2 minutes. Gradually stir in cream, increase heat slightly, and simmer until sauce is thickened and bubbly.

Add all remaining ingredients except cheeses; stir to blend. Pour into a 2-quart greased baking dish, greased baking shells or individual greased casseroles, and sprinkle with cheese. Bake for 20 minutes. Serve with steamed rice.

Serves 6

Serve with Merlot.

Broiled Salmon Teriyaki

MARINADE

¼	**cup soy sauce**
¼	**cup rice vinegar**
¼	**cup lemon juice**
¼	**Merlot wine**
1	**tablespoon granulated sugar**
1	**tablespoon olive oil**
1	**teaspoon dry mustard**
1	**teaspoon ground ginger**
¼	**teaspoon sea salt or kosher salt**
1½	**teaspoons cornstarch (add after broiling fish)**

4	**salmon fillets (about 1 pound), boned and skinned**
1	**green onion, finely sliced, for garnish**

Combine all marinade ingredients except cornstarch and stir to blend. Place salmon fillets in a shallow dish, and pour marinade over fish. Cover and let stand at room temperature for 30 minutes, turning once, or cover and refrigerate for up to 1 hour, turning occasionally. Remove fish from marinade, reserving marinade.

Place salmon on unheated rack of broiler pan. Broil 4 inches from heat for 4 to 6 minutes per ½-inch thickness of salmon, turning and brushing with marinade once halfway through. Transfer to serving platter and keep warm.

Combine remaining marinade with Merlot to equal ½ cup. In a small saucepan, stir 1½ teaspoons cornstarch into marinade mixture. Cook and stir until thickened and bubbly. Cook 1 minute more. Spoon over salmon fillets. Garnish with green onion.

Serves 4

Serve with Merlot.

Crab with Mushrooms and Merlot

2	tablespoons butter
1	tablespoon finely chopped onion
1	cup sliced fresh mushrooms
½	cup finely chopped water chestnuts
½	cup finely chopped celery
1	tablespoon green bell pepper
1	tablespoon fresh chopped parsley
2	tablespoons flour
2½	cups half and half milk
2	cups diced crab meat
2	egg yolks
¼	cup Merlot wine

In a large saucepan over medium heat, melt butter and add onion, mushrooms, water chestnuts, celery, green pepper, and parsley; cover and cook gently, stirring frequently, for 10 minutes.

Blend flour into onion-mushroom mixture; add 2 cups of the half and half milk; cook, stirring continuously, until mixture has thickened and is smooth. Add salt, pepper, and crab.

Beat egg yolks, add remaining half and half, and blend well. Add milk mixture and Merlot to crab mixture; stir. Adjust seasonings to taste. Cook 1 minute. Serve immediately on rice, in patty shells, or on toast.

Serves 6

Serve with Merlot.

65

Super Shrimp Casserole

¼   cup butter
¾   cup Merlot wine
1   clove garlic, minced
1   pound fresh mushrooms, sliced
1   pound cooked shrimp
2   cups cooked rice
1   cup half and half
¼   cup chili sauce
¼   cup lemon juice
1   tablespoon Worcestershire sauce
1   teaspoon sea salt or kosher salt
½   teaspoon freshly ground pepper
1   cup grated Parmesan or Romano cheese

Preheat oven to 350° F.

In a large skillet over medium-high heat, melt butter, and stir in Merlot, garlic and mushrooms; sauté until liquid is reduced by about half. Stir in shrimp and rice.

In a medium-sized bowl, combine half and half, chili sauce, lemon juice, Worcestershire sauce, salt and pepper; add to

mushroom mixture and stir well. Pour into a greased casserole, sprinkle with grated cheese, and bake for 35 to 45 minutes, or until heated through and bubbly.

Serves 8

Serve with Merlot.

Oysters with Merlot

3	tablespoons butter
1	small onion, finely chopped
1	clove garlic, minced
1	small carrot, pared and thinly sliced
½	cup diced celery
3½	tablespoons flour
2¼	cups hot chicken stock
½	cup Merlot wine
¼	cup fresh shredded basil, firmly packed
1	teaspoon sea salt or kosher salt
½	teaspoon black pepper
	Tabasco sauce to taste
1¾	cups cooked oysters, shucked
½	cup grated Gruyère cheese

In a medium-sized saucepan of over medium-high heat, melt butter, and stir in onion, garlic, carrot, and celery. Cover and cook for 5 minutes.

Decrease heat to low. Add flour to butter-vegetable mixture and stir well; cook 1 minute. Slowly add chicken stock and Merlot, stirring continuously. Add basil, salt, pepper, and Tabasco sauce. Cook, uncovered, 7 or 8 minutes longer over low heat. Stir in oysters and simmer for 2 to 3 minutes.

Spoon into individual casseroles or scallop shells, top with cheese and put under broiler for several minutes to melt cheese.

Serves 4

Serve with Merlot.

Sweet and Sour Seafood

SWEET & SOUR SAUCE
1   tablespoon cornstarch
¼   cup granulated sugar
½   cup Merlot wine
¼   cup lemon juice
¼   cup chicken broth
2   tablespoons soy sauce
1   tablespoon catsup

SEAFOOD
¼   cup cornstarch
2   pounds halibut fillets, or other favorite fish, cut into
     2-inch squares
2   cloves garlic, minced
1   small onion, cut into bite-sized pieces
1   small green bell pepper, cut into bite-sized pieces
1   small red bell pepper, cut into bite-sized pieces
1   large tomato, cut into bite-sized pieces
½   cup sliced water chestnuts
     Capers and lemon slices for garnish

In a small bowl, combine 1 tablespoon cornstarch with sugar, Merlot, lemon juice, chicken broth, soy sauce, and catsup. Set aside.

In a plastic bag, add ¼ cup cornstarch and fish pieces; shake gently to coat completely. Shake excess cornstarch from fish.

In a large skillet, pour cooking oil to a depth of about ¼ inch. Turn heat to medium-high. When oil is hot, add halibut fillets, a few pieces at a time, and cook until fish is browned on all sides and flesh flakes easily with a fork, about 5 minutes. Drain fish on paper towels; transfer to a serving platter and keep warm.

In a small saucepan, heat 2 tablespoons cooking oil over medium-high heat. Add garlic, onion, peppers, and water chestnuts. Sauté, stirring frequently, for about 2 minutes.

Stir sweet-and-sour sauce and add to vegetable mixture. Add tomato. Cook, stirring continuously, until mixture comes to a boil. Pour immediately over fish. Garnish with capers and lemon slices.

Serves 4 to 6

Serve with Merlot.

Suzette's Swift Shrimp

¼   **cup butter**
2   **10½-ounce cans condensed cream of mushroom soup**
1   **cup half and half or whole milk**
2   **teaspoons minced chives**
2   **teaspoons minced parsley**
½   **teaspoon paprika**
¼   **cup Merlot wine**
1   **pound medium-sized shrimp, shelled and deveined**
2   **hard-boiled eggs, finely chopped**

In a large saucepan over low heat, combine all ingredients in order given. Heat thoroughly, stirring so that ingredients are well blended. Adjust seasonings to taste. Serve with rice or over toast. Sprinkle with additional paprika.

Serves 6

Serve with Merlot.

Fisherman's Barbecued Salmon Merlot

½   cup olive oil
4   salmon fillets
1   cup Merlot wine
2   tablespoons dried oregano flakes
     Juice of 1 lemon
1   tablespoon dried dill weed
1   teaspoon sea salt or kosher salt
½   teaspoon fresh ground black pepper
     Worcestershire sauce

Fire up the barbecue grill.

Using heavy aluminum foil, make a sturdy "boat" (pan) with 3-inch high sides, slightly longer and wider than the salmon to be cooked. Generously coat the inside of the boat with olive oil and lay the salmon fillets in it. Over each fillet pour Merlot, then sprinkle with oregano, salt and pepper, lemon juice, dill weed, and a dash of Worcestershire sauce.

Put the boat with salmon fillets and sauce on the barbecue grill; simmer for 20 minutes, turning fish every 5 minutes.

Remove salmon fillets from foil boat/pan and place directly on barbecue grill; grill for 1 to 1½ minutes per side.

Serve with fresh lemon wedges.

Serves 4

Serve with Merlot.

70

Three-Fish Teriyaki

½   cup bottled teriyaki sauce
½   cup Merlot wine
1½ teaspoons finely chopped fresh ginger or ¾ teaspoon ground ginger
2   cloves garlic, minced
2½ teaspoons cornstarch
½   pound medium-sized raw shrimp, shelled and deveined
½   pound scallops, cut into bite-sized pieces
½   pound fresh crabmeat, cut into bite-sized pieces
¼   cup peanut oil
¼   pound fresh pea pods
½   pound mushrooms, sliced
6   green onions, cut into 2-inch lengths
1   small can sliced water chestnuts

In a deep bowl, combine teriyaki sauce, Merlot, ginger, garlic and cornstarch; add shrimp, scallops, and crabmeat. Cover and refrigerate for 30 minutes to 2 hours.

Using a large skillet or wok, heat 3 tablespoons of the oil over high heat. When oil is hot, add pea pods; cook, stirring rapidly, until pea pods are bright green. Remove from skillet and set aside.

Add remaining oil to skillet or wok. When hot, add mushrooms; cook and stir until soft, 2 to 3 minutes. Add seafood mixture, green onions, and water chestnuts; cook, stirring frequently, just until shrimp turns pink. Stir in pea pod mixture and serve immediately with rice.

Serves 4 to 6

Serve with Merlot.

Seafood Sampler with Tomatoes

¼	cup butter
1	clove garlic, minced
1	cup fresh mushrooms, sliced
¾	pound scallops
½	pound crabmeat
½	pound shrimp, peeled and deveined
¾	cup Merlot wine
2	tablespoons lemon juice
1	teaspoon sea salt or kosher salt
½	teaspoon black pepper
1	28-ounce can tomatoes, drained and chopped
2	tablespoons tomato paste
1	tablespoon chopped parsley
½	cup grated Gruyère cheese

In a large skillet over medium heat, melt butter. Add garlic, mushrooms, scallops, crabmeat, shrimp, Merlot, lemon juice, salt and pepper. Cook for 3 to 4 minutes, stirring frequently. Add tomatoes and simmer for 2 to 3 minutes. Stir in tomato paste and cook 1 minute more. Adjust seasoning to taste.

Pour mixture into a large ovenproof dish. Top with parsley and cheese. Broil in oven until golden brown.

Serve in individual casseroles or scallop shells.

Serves 4

Serve with Merlot.

Sautéed Rainbow Trout in Tangy Merlot-Blue Cheese Sauce

4	6- to 8-inch trout
¾	cup butter, divided into ½ cup and ¼ cup portions
½	cup fresh mushrooms, sliced
½	cup Merlot wine
2	shallots, minced
½	teaspoon balsamic vinegar
2	tablespoons blue cheese
1	teaspoon sea salt or kosher salt
½	teaspoon black pepper
1	teaspoon lemon juice

In a large skillet over medium heat, melt ½ cup butter and sauté mushrooms until tender; set aside. In the same skillet, fry trout, one side at a time, until the skin is crisp and golden. Remove trout to a serving platter and keep warm.

Add the Merlot to the skillet and deglaze by stirring together the wine and remaining browned bits of trout from the bottom of the skillet. Add the shallots and balsamic vinegar and, stirring continuously, reduce the mixture to a glaze.

Remove the skillet from heat and immediately whisk in ¼ cup butter until melted. Add blue cheese and continue whisking until sauce is smooth. Add salt, pepper and lemon juice. Adjust seasonings to taste. Pour the Merlot-blue cheese sauce over the trout and serve.

Serves 4

Delicious with Merlot.

73

Broiled Tuna Steaks with Merlot Sauce

4   **6-ounce tuna steaks, 1-inch thick**

MARINADE   **3**   **tablespoons soy sauce**
                          3   **tablespoons sesame oil**
                          ¼   **cup dry sherry**
                          1   **teaspoon grated orange zest**

SAUCE   **3**   **teaspoons lemon juice**
                          ½   **cup Merlot wine**
                          1   **tablespoon fresh minced ginger**
                          1½ sticks butter, cut into ¼-inch pieces
                          1   **tablespoon capers**
                          ½   **teaspoon dry dill weed**

Place tuna steaks in a large glass dish. Combine soy sauce, sesame oil, dry sherry and orange zest; pour over steaks. Refrigerate for a minimum of one hour, turning steaks several times while they are marinating.

Just before broiling steaks, make the sauce. Combine lemon juice, Merlot, and ginger in a nonreactive saucepan and cook until liquid is reduced by half. Remove from heat and whisk in butter, one piece at a time. Return saucepan to low heat and continue whisking until butter is melted. Stir in capers and dill weed. Keep warm.

Broil tuna for 2 to 3 minutes per side or until cooked to taste. Spoon sauce over steaks and serve.

Serves 4

Serve with Merlot.

Desserts

Strawberries in Merlot

This simple dessert is absolutely delicious! Macadamia nuts and Merlot are excellent together.

3   cups (about 1 pound) fresh sliced strawberries
½   cup Merlot wine, chilled
¼   cup granulated sugar
½   cup whipped cream
½   cup finely chopped Macadamia nuts
**   Fresh mint or basil leaves for garnish**

Sprinkle strawberries with sugar, refrigerate, and let stand for 2 hours before serving.

To serve, place strawberries and some of the wine syrup marinade in individual chilled dessert dishes. Pour the chilled Merlot over strawberries, top with whipped cream and sprinkle liberally with Macadamia nuts.

Serves 4

Serve with Merlot.

English Tipsy Trifle

4   layers (9-inch round) sponge or angel food cake, from mix, scratch or store
1   13-ounce package vanilla pudding mix (not instant)
1½ cups milk
1   teaspoon grated lemon peel
2   cups heavy cream
¼   cup granulated sugar
2   teaspoons vanilla
½   cup Merlot wine
1   cup strawberry jam or preserves, well chilled
      Whole strawberries

If baking cake layers, mix according to recipe or package directions and bake about 25 minutes. Cool and refrigerate.

Cook vanilla pudding according to package directions using 1½ cups milk. Add lemon peel. Place plastic wrap directly on surface of pudding. Cool.

Combine heavy cream and sugar; whip until stiff. Add vanilla, stir, and fold into cooled pudding. Refrigerate.

Place one cake layer on a large serving plate; sprinkle cake with 2 tablespoons Merlot wine. Spread with 2 to 3 tablespoons chilled jam and pudding custard. Repeat with second and third layers of cake. On top layer, drizzle last of Merlot and spread with jam.

Frost sides of cake with whipped cream; leave jam on top uncovered. Decorate top with whole strawberries set in jam.

Serves 10 to 12

Serve with Merlot.

Flaming Cherries

2   pounds Bing cherries, pitted; or use canned Bing cherries, drained
2   cups Merlot wine
8   tablespoons sugar
¼   teaspoon cinnamon
1   teaspoon cornstarch
1½   tablespoons blackberry jelly
3   ounces kirsch or dark rum

Place cherries in saucepan with wine, sugar and cinnamon. Bring to a boil and cook for 3 minutes. Drain and place in hot baking dish.

Cook wine and sugar mixture until it is reduced to ¾ cup. Blend in cornstarch and jelly. Remove from stove and add to cherry mixture. Sprinkle with kirsch or rum. Bring to the table and light with a match or butane lighter stick.

Serves 6 to 8

Serve with Merlot.

78

Chocolate Merlot Cake

1	cup butter
1	cup granulated sugar
2	eggs
1	teaspoon vanilla extract
1	teaspoon almond extract
1	package (12 ounces) semisweet chocolate chips
2	teaspoons baking powder
2¼	cups all-purpose flour
½	cup Merlot wine
4	tablespoons unsweetened cocoa powder
	Buttercream frosting, if desired
	Sliced almond for garnish, if desired

Preheat oven to 325° F.

In a large bowl, mix butter, sugar, and eggs until smooth and creamy; add vanilla and almond extracts and chocolate chips; mix well.

In a small bowl, combine baking powder and flour; add to creamed mixture. Add Merlot and combine with a few strokes. Add cocoa powder. Pour into a greased 9-inch cake pan.

Bake for 45 minutes to 1 hour, until top of cake springs back when lightly touched. Cool. Frost with buttercream frosting sprinkled with almonds. Or, serve unfrosted with fresh strawberries, chocolate sauce and whipped cream.

Serves 6 to 8

Serve with Merlot.

79

Baked Apples Merlot

8   apples, cored
2   8-ounce jars cherry or strawberry jam
½   cup granulated sugar
½   teaspoon mace
½   teaspoon nutmeg
½   cup raisins
1   cup Merlot wine
½   teaspoon vanilla flavoring
1   cup sour cream
2   tablespoons powdered sugar
1   cup chopped pecans, walnuts or almonds

Preheat oven to 350° F.

Butter a shallow, 8 x 12-inch baking dish, place apples in it, and fill each apple with jam, reserving remaining jam.

In a medium-sized bowl, combine sugar, mace, and nutmeg. Add raisins, wine, and vanilla flavoring; stir. Pour over apples and cover. Bake for 1 hour. Refrigerate for 2 to 4 hours before serving.

Combine sour cream and powdered sugar; chill.

To serve, warm remaining jam to a liquid state in a small saucepan. Spoon a small portion of jam onto each individual serving plate, place a baked apple on jam, top with a dollop of the sour cream mixture, and sprinkle with chopped nuts.

Serves 8

Serve with Merlot.

Peaches in Merlot

2	**pounds ripe peaches**
2	**cups Merlot wine**
½	**cup granulated sugar**
1	**vanilla bean, split**
¼	**cup whole roasted almonds, shelled**
½	**cup white raisins**
1	**tablespoon fresh mint, finely shredded**

Fill a large bowl with ice water; set aside.

Fill a large saucepan about ⅔ full of water and bring to a boil. Plunge peaches, a few at a time, into the boiling water for about 1 minute. Remove peaches from boiling water and plunge into bowl of ice water for about 1 minute. Using your hands, remove peach skins. Slice peaches in half and remove pits.

In a small saucepan, heat Merlot, sugar and vanilla bean. Bring to a boil and simmer for 3 minutes.

Place peaches, almonds and raisins in a bowl. Pour the hot Merlot sauce over all. Set aside until peach mixture returns to room temperature, about 30 minutes.

To serve, sprinkle with mint

Serves 4

Serve with Merlot.

81

Black Forest Brownies

½   cup butter
4   ounces unsweetened chocolate
4   eggs
2   cups sugar
1   tablespoon Merlot wine
2   teaspoons cinnamon
½   teaspoon nutmeg
1¼ cups flour
½   teaspoon salt
1   cup chopped walnuts
1   cup chopped glazed cherries

Preheat oven to 350° F. Melt butter and chocolate in a small saucepan. Let cool.

Break eggs into a large bowl and beat. Add sugar, Merlot, cinnamon and nutmeg. Mix well. Gradually add flour and salt, and beat until smooth. Blend in chocolate mixture. Add walnuts and cherries.

Spread mixture in a 9 x 13-inch greased cake pan. Bake for 35 minutes. Cool completely. Cut into 2-inch squares.

Makes approximately 24 brownies

Serve with Merlot.

Marinated Grape Delight
Simple to prepare and simply delicious!

1	pound seedless green grapes
¼	cup Merlot wine
¼	cup honey
1	teaspoon lemon juice
1	8-ounce container sour cream or 8 ounces of yogurt or whipped cream
½	cup dark brown sugar, firmly packed Mint leaves for garnish

Rinse grapes; drain.

In a separate bowl, stir together the Merlot, honey and lemon juice. Pour this mixture over the grapes and marinate 2 to 6 hours or overnight.

Prior to serving, combine sour cream and brown sugar. Stir until sugar melts and mixture is thoroughly blended.

To serve, divide grapes into 4 chilled dessert dishes. Spoon sour cream mixture over grapes and garnish with mint leaves.

Serves 4

Serve with Merlot.

Quick Chocolate Mousse Merlot

1	cup heavy cream
½	cup powdered sugar
½	cup granulated sugar
¼	cup water
2	eggs
1	6-ounce package semisweet chocolate morsels
2	tablespoons granulated sugar
1	teaspoon espresso or other dark coffee
3	tablespoons Merlot wine
	chocolate sprinkles for garnish

Whip cream and powdered sugar until soft peaks form. Chill.

In a small saucepan, heat sugar and water until sugar dissolves. Simmer for 2 minutes. Remove from heat.

Combine eggs and chocolate in a food processor or blender. Add granulated sugar to chocolate mixture while machine is running. Process or blend for 2 minutes. Add coffee and Merlot and mix for 30 seconds more.

Fold chocolate mixture into whipped cream. Pour into individual dessert dishes or goblets, or into a 1-quart container, and refrigerate for several hours or overnight. Garnish with chocolate sprinkles.

Serves 6

Serve with Merlot.

Merlot Plum Pudding

¾   cup Merlot wine
1½   pounds dark-skinned plums, fully ripe
⅔   cup granulated sugar
1   teaspoon vanilla extract
½   teaspoon lemon juice
4   teaspoons (about 1½ envelopes) unflavored gelatin
¼   cup water
2   cups whipped cream or sweetened sour cream

Rinse and slice plums. In a medium-sized saucepan, combine the Merlot wine with the plums and simmer, covered, pits and all, until plums are soft, about 20 minutes.

Remove pits from cooked plums. Measure 3 cups of the plum pulp and liquid; set aside. Using a food processor or blender, purée pulp until it is smooth. Add sugar, vanilla, and lemon juice. Blend thoroughly until sugar is dissolved.

In a small saucepan, add water, sprinkle gelatin over water, and soak until gelatin is soft, about 5 minutes. Over very low heat, stir the gelatin until it melts; stir into the plum purée.

Rinse a 4-cup mold (or individual molds) with cold water, and pour the plum mixture into it. Chill the plum pudding until it is firm, 2 to 6 hours or longer. To serve, unmold by briefly dipping the mold up to the rim in hot water and turning onto a dessert plate. Top with whipped cream or sweetened sour cream.

Serves 6 to 8

Serve with Merlot.

Rhubard Crisp with Merlot

2	cups sliced fresh rhubarb or frozen unsweetened sliced rhubarb, thawed
2	cups sliced strawberries
2	tablespoons snipped fresh basil or 1½ teaspoon dried basil, crumbled
¼	cup Merlot wine
1	cup granulated sugar
1	tablespoon cornstarch
¼	teaspoon ground cinnamon
¼	teaspoon ground nutmeg
½	cup all-purpose flour
½	cup quick-cooking oats
½	cup chopped walnuts or other nut meats
¼	cup packed brown sugar
¼	teaspoon salt
2	tablespoons butter, melted

Preheat oven to 375° F. In a medium-sized bowl combine rhubarb, strawberries, basil and Merlot wine. Add granulated sugar, cornstarch, cinnamon, and nutmeg. Stir well and spoon into the bottom of a greased 8 x 8 x 2-inch baking dish. Set aside.

In a separate bowl, combine flour, oats, nuts, brown sugar and salt. Stir in melted butter. Sprinkle over fruit mixture. Bake for 30 to 35 minutes or until fruit is tender and topping is golden brown.

Delicious topped with vanilla ice cream.

Serves 6

Serve with Merlot.

Cranberry, Raisin and Nut Pie

Pastry for a 2-crust pie
2   cups (about 1½ pounds) fresh or frozen cranberries
2   cups dark raisins
1   cup chopped walnuts or pecans
2   tablespoons water
2   teaspoons lemon juice
½   cup Merlot wine
1¹/₃ cups granulated sugar
2   tablespoons flour
½   teaspoon ground cardamom seeds
½   teaspoon mace
Light cream or evaporated milk for glaze

Preheat oven to 450° F. In a food processor, coarsely chop cranberries, raisins and nuts. Blend in water, lemon juice and Merlot. In a separate bowl, stir together the sugar, flour, cardamom and mace; stir into pie filling.

Pour cranberry filling into the pastry-lined pan, cover with top crust, trim, seal, crimp edges. Cut vents in top crust, then brush lightly with cream. Bake for 10 minutes at 450° F, then lower heat to 350° F and continue baking for about 40 minutes, or until top crust has browned sufficiently and some juice bubbles through vent slits. Cool and serve.

Serves 6 to 8

Serve with Merlot.

Glossary and Pronunciation Guide

Al dente (al DEN-tee; al-DEN-tay): A term for pasta that is cooked until tender but not soft, having a firmness that is somewhat resistant to the teeth. Literally, "to the tooth" in Italian.

Arrowroot): A tasteless, starchy powder derived from the tropical arrowroot tuber, used to thicken cooked foods. It has twice the thickening power of wheat flour, and, unlike cornstarch, does not taste chalky when undercooked.

Asiago (Ah-see-AH-go): A yellow cheese suitable for grating when aged, from Asiago, Italy.

Au Gratin (oh GRAHT-n): Food cooked with a top crust of bread crumbs and butter, sauce or grated cheese, and then browned in an oven.

Basil (BAYZ-l): A sweet, aromatic herb in the mint family that is cultivated for its leaves. When purchased fresh and not used immediately, basil will maintain its quality longer if it is placed in a container of water, stem ends down like a bouquet, and kept in the refrigerator. Basil is a main ingredient in pesto and is a popular seasoning in many modern recipes.

To baste (BAY-st): The process of spooning melted butter, hot fat, a sauce, or other liquid over meat as it roasts to keep it moist and juicy.

Bay leaf: The dried, aromatic leaf of the laurel or bay tree. It is normally used in a dried state as a flavoring for soups, stews, meats and other dishes, removed from the food prior to serving.

To beat: To stir rapidly with a circular motion, using a spoon, whisk, rotary beater or electric mixer, to give lightness to a mixture. Approximately 100 strokes by hand equals 1 minute by electric mixer.

Bisque (BISK): A rich, creamy soup made from fish, shellfish, meat, or puréed vegetables.

To blanch: To plunge food (usually fruits and vegetables) into boiling water briefly, then into cold water to stop the cooking process. Blanching is generally used to partially cook foods before adding them to certain dishes, or to loosen the skin (as with tomatoes or peaches) for easy removal.

To blend: To stir a mixture until the ingredients are completely combined and smooth.

Blue cheese: A type of cheese that has been treated with molds that form blue or green veins throughout and give the cheese its characteristic strong flavor and aroma, both of which intensify with aging.

To boil: To immerse food in water, stock or other liquid when it has reached 212° F and is bubbling vigorously.

Bouillon (BOOL-yon; BOO-yon): A clear, thin broth made by simmering beef, chicken or vegetables with seasonings.

Bouillon (BOOL-yon) cube: A small cube of evaporated seasoned meat, poultry or vegetable stock used to make broth or add flavor to soups, stews and other dishes. Bouillon cubes are packed in small containers and sold in grocery stores.

Bouquet garni (boh-kay gar-nee): Herbs (traditionally 2 or 3 stalks of parsley, a sprig of thyme, and a bay leaf) tied together with string, wrapped in cheesecloth, or enclosed in a small cloth sack, then immersed in soups and stews to add flavor. The bouquet is removed from the cooked food before serving.

To braise (brayz): To brown meat, vegetables, or other foods in hot fat, then cook them in a small amount of liquid in a tightly covered container at low heat for an extended period of time. Braising can be done on the stove top or in the oven.

Butterfly (cut): To cut or split a food (such as leg of lamb or shrimp) down the center, cutting almost through. The two halves are then opened flat, resembling a butterfly shape.

Cacciatore (kah-chah-TOR-ee): Italian dishes prepared with tomatoes, mushrooms, onions, herbs and, often, wine. Literally, "hunter" in Italian, this American-Italian term refers to foods prepared in the hearty style of hunters.

Caper (KAY-per): A pickled flower bud of the caper bush. Packed in salt or vinegar and sold in grocery stores, the pungent condiment is used in sauces, relishes, and many other dishes.

Cardamom (KAHR-deh-mehm)(-mehn): The seeds of an Indian herb fruit, used as a spice or condiment.

Casserole (KAS-eh-rohl): A dish, usually of earthenware or glass, in which food is baked and served. Both the container and the food prepared in it are referred to as a casserole.

Cheddar cheese: Any of several types of firm, smooth cheese made from cow's milk. Cheddar ranges in flavor from mild to extra sharp and is naturally white but is often colored with a natural orange dye. This popular cheese originated in the village of Cheddar in the Somerset region of England.

Chervil (CHUR-vl): A delicate fernlike herb often used to flavor sauces and vinegars (often in combination with tarragon) and as a garnish. A member of the parsley family, chervil leaves are sweeter and more aromatic than standard parsley.

Chives (ch-eye-vs): The leaves of a bulbous herb of the lily family used as seasoning.

Chowder: A thick soup containing fish or shellfish and vegetables in a milk or tomato base. Or, a soup similar to this seafood dish.

Cilantro (see-LAHN-troh): The Spanish name for coriander, from old Spanish alteration of the Latin *coriandrum*. It is widely used in Asian, Caribbean and Latin American cooking.

Coq au Vin (kohk-oh-VAHN): A classic French dish made of chicken, bacon or pork, onions, herbs and red wine.

Coquilles St. Jacques: (koh-KEEL sahn-ZHAHK, koh-KEE sahn-ZHAHK): A classic dish consisting of scallops in a creamy wine sauce, topped with bread crumbs or cheese and browned under a broiler, typically served in a scallop shell.

Coriander (KOHR-ee-an-der): An aromatic herb in the parsley family. The fresh, pungent leaves of this plant (also called Chinese parsley and cilantro) are used in salads and other, especially highly seasoned. The seedlike fruit, used whole or ground, is used as a seasoning, as in curry powder.

Cornstarch: A very fine flour made from corn, largely used as a thickening agent.

Crisp-tender: Vegetables that are cooked until they are tender but not soft, having a fresh crispness that is somewhat resistent to the teeth.

Cumin (KOO-mihn): A dried fruit of a plant in the parsley family whose aromatic, nutty-flavored seeds, which are available in seed and ground forms, are popular in Asian, Mediterranean and Middle Eastern cooking. .

Curry powder: A pungent seasoning blended from chili, cinnamon, cumin, coriander, ginger, mustard, pepper, turmeric, and other spices. Curry powders are available from mild to hot depending on the amount of hotter spices used in the blend.

Deglaze (dee-GLAYZ): To dissolve the remaining bits of sautéed meat or roasted food and congealed juices from the bottom of a pan by adding a liquid and heating. First, the food is removed and excess fat discarded, then the remaining sediments are heated with stock, wine, or other liquid to make a gravy or sauce.

Dollop (DOLL-ehp): A small quantity or splash of a food substance.

Dredge (DREJ): To coat food by sprinkling it with flour, sugar, bread crumbs, or other powdery mixture or substance.

Feta (FEHT-ah): A semisoft white cheese usually made from goat's or ewe's milk and often preserved in brine, which gives it a slightly astringent and salty flavor. From the modern Greek *pheta*, "slice of cheese," and the Italian *fetta*, "slice."

Fennel (FEN-l): A Eurasian plant and its edible seeds or stalks, which have an anise flavor and are used to season foods.

Fettucine (FET-eh-CHEE-nee): Pasta cut into narrow flat strips, or a dish made with this pasta.

Fines herbes (feen ZEHRB, feen ehrb) : A classic blend of finely chopped herbs, specifically chervil, chives, parsley, tarragon, and thyme, mixed together and used as a seasoning. Literally, "fine herbs" in French.

To garnish: To decorate prepared foods or beverages with small, colorful or savory items such as parsley, chopped scallions, flowers, mint leaves, or nuts.

Green onion/scallion: An immature onion harvested before the bulb has developed. Both the green stem and the immature white bulb are delicious and can be used in recipes.

Gruyère (groo-YEHR): A nutty, pale yellow, firm cheese made from cow's milk, named for its area of origin in Switzerland.

Italian (ih-tal-yen): From or characteristic of Italy. The "I" in "Italian" is pronounced like the "I" in "Italy" (IH-tal-ee).

Jack cheese (also known as California Jack, Monterey Jack, and Sonoma Jack): A versatile cheese made from cow's milk. **Unaged Jack** is ivory colored, semisoft in texture, and mildly flavored. It is widely available throughout the United States, plain or flavored with jalapeño pepper, garlic, dill or other seasonings. **Aged or Dry Jack** is yellow colored, firm textured, and sharper flavored and is generally found only on the West Coast or in specialty cheese shops.

Jalapeño (ha-la-PEN-yo): A spicy red or green pepper.

Kosher salt: A refined, coarse-grained salt that has no additives.

Lasagna, lasagne (luh-ZAHN-yuh): A wide, flat noodle, sometimes with ruffled edges. Also, a baked dish made by layering lasagna noodles with cheeses, fillings, and sauce.

Leek: A plant related to the onion.

Linguine/linguini (lin-GWEE-nee): Pasta cut into long, flat, thin strands.

Macaroni (mac-ah-ROH-nee): Any of several types of hollow pasta, especially short curved tubes.

Mace (may-s): An aromatic spice derived from the dried, lacy, outer coating of the nutmeg kernel. Mace and nutmeg can be used interchangeably.

Maraschino (mar-ah-SKEE-no) cherries: Sweet pitted cherries that are tinted with red food coloring and preserved in a sugar syrup. The name is derived from the Italian marasca cherry and the maraschino cordial made from the cherry's fermented juice and crushed pits.

Marjoram (MAR-jer-em): A spicy aromatic herb whose leaves are used for seasoning, especially popular in bread stuffing and with lamb.

Marinade (MARE-eh-nayd): A liquid combination, usually vinegar or wine, oil, and various herbs and spices, in which meat or vegetables are soaked before cooking.

Merlot (mer-LOH): A very popular dry red wine made from the Merlot grape. (See the introduction for more details.)

Mousse (MOOS): A rich, light, airy dish that takes its name from the French word for "froth" or "foam." A mousse can be a chilled, sweet dessert or a hot, savory dish. Fluffiness results from adding whipped cream or beaten egg whites.

Mozzarella (mot-seh-REL-eh): A mild, white Italian cheese with a rubbery texture, often eaten melted on pizza and in Italian dishes. From the Italian *mozzare*, "to cut off."

Nutmeg: A sweet, nutty spice derived from the seed of the East Indies nutmeg tree. Grated or ground, nutmeg is popularly used in cakes, cookies, custards and white sauces.

Orzo (OHR-zoh): A tiny, rice-shaped pasta that is excellent in soups and when served as a side dish. Literally, "barley" in Italian

Pancetta (pan-CHET-ah): Italian bacon that has been cured in salt and spices and then air-dried.

To pare: To remove a very thin layer from the outer covering or skin of fruits or vegetables with a knife or vegetable peeler.

Parmesan (PAR-meh-zahn): A hard, sharp, dry Italian cheese made from skim milk. Its dry texture is ideal for grating or as a garnish. It originated in Parma, Italy.

Pesto (PES-toh): A tangy sauce made with fresh basil, garlic, pine nuts, olive oil, and grated Parmesan cheese, generally used on pasta, in soups or stews, and as a dip.

Pilaf (pih-LAHF; PEE-lahf): A steamed rice dish often made with meat, seafood or vegetables in a seasoned broth.

Piquant (PEE-kehnt; pee-KAHNT): Tasting pleasantly spicy, pungent or tart. From the Old French *piquer*, "to prick."

Pit: The single hard seed, kernel or stone of certain fruits, such as those in apricots, cherries, or peaches. / **To pit:** To remove seeds or stones from fruit.

To poach: To cook gently in simmering liquid so that the cooked food retains its shape.

Proscuitto (pro-SHOO-toh): An aged, dry, spicy Italian ham that is usually sliced thin and served without cooking.

Purée (pyoo-RAY): Fruit, vegetables, meat or other food (usually precooked) that is rubbed through a strainer, sieved, or blended in a food processor to a thick cream.

Ragout (ra-GOO): A stew in which the meat is usually browned before stewing, made from pieces of meat or fish that are cooked slowly without thickening.

To reduce: To diminish the quantity and improve the quality of a sauce or other cooking liquid by gently boiling until it becomes thicker and the flavor more concentrated.

Ricotta (rih-KAHT-ah): A soft, bland, fresh cheese that resembles cottage cheese, popularly used in lasagna, canneloni, and other Italian dishes. From the Latin *rococta* and *recoquere*, "to cook again."

Romano (roh-MAH-noh) cheese: A very firm, pale yellow cheese generally used in a grated form. Named for the city of Rome in which they originated, there are several different styles of Romano cheese, made with sheep's, goat's, or cow's milk and varying from mild to very sharp.

Roux (ROO): A fat-and-flour mixture that is cooked together and used to thicken sauces. There are three types of roux – white, blond and brown. White roux is not cooked after the flour is added, blond roux is cooked until straw-colored, and brown roux is cooked until it is a dark brown color.

Sage (SAYJ): Any of several native Mediterranean plants with grayish-green, aromatic leaves that are used as seasonings, commonly in dishes containing pork, cheese and beans, and in poultry and game stuffings.

Sauerbraten (SOUR-BRAHT-n): A pot roast marinated in vinegar, water, wine, and spices before cooking to give it a distinctive sharp flavor. Literally, "sour roast" in German.

To sauté (saw-TAY): To fry foods lightly in fat in a shallow open pan. Also, sauté refers to any dish prepared in this manner.

Scallion/green onion: An immature onion harvested before the bulb has developed. Both the green stem and the immature white bulb are delicious and can be used in recipes.

Scallops: Small, white shellfish that grow in fan-shaped shells with a radiating fluted pattern. 1) **Bay scallops** have a sweet, nutlike flavor and are relatively scarce; 2) **sea scallops** have a robust taste and are more widely available.

Sea salt: Salt produced by the evaporation of sea water and that contains sodium chloride and trace elements such as sulfur, magnesium, zinc, potassium, calcium, and iron, generally used in a coarse state.

Seasoning: Salt, pepper, herbs and other flavorings used in cooking. To "adjust" or "correct" seasoning is to taste the food near the end of the cooking period to see seasonings are needed, then to add more to suit your taste.

Serrano (seh-RRAH-noh) chili: A small chile with a very hot, savory flavor. It is available fresh, canned, pickled, packed in oil, and dried (*chile seco*).

Shallot (SHALL-et): A type of onion whose mild-flavored bulb is used in soups, sauces, stews, and other dishes. Shallots grow like garlic in a cluster on a common vine.

Simmer: To cook liquid gently at about 195° F or remain just at or below the liquid's boiling point.

Spaghetti squash: A creamy yellow, oblong squash with flesh that, when cooked, separates into golden spaghettilike strands that can be served with pasta sauce or used in various dishes.

To steam: To cook food by placing it on a rack in a closed container and exposing the food to moist steam heat (pressurized water vapor), being careful to keep the food away from boiling water below it.

Stock: A broth made by simmering meat, bones, poultry, vegetables or fish for several hours, used as a base in preparing soup, stew, gravy, or sauces.

Stuffing, dressing: A mixture of savory ingredients, usually highly seasoned, used to fill cavities in fish, poultry, or meat, or cooked separately. Although the terms are often used interchangeably, more precisely, *stuffing* is cooked inside the meat, fish, or poultry; *dressing* is cooked in a dish or pan.

Sun-dried tomatoes: Tomatoes that are dried in the sun (or by artificial methods), which intensifies their flavor, sweetness, and color. They are chewy (like dried fruit), and are usually packed in oil or dry-packed in cellophane. Sun-dried tomatoes add delicious flavor dimensions to a wide variety of dishes.

Swiss cheese: A firm white or pale yellow cheese with a nutlike flavor and many holes, originally produced in Switzerland.

Tabasco (tah-BAS-koh) sauce: Any sauce made from spicy, strong-flavored tabasco peppers. Tabasco is also a trademarked brand name.

Thyme (TYME): Any of several aromatic herbs whose leaves are used in *bouquet garni* and as a seasoning in soups, vegetables, stews, poultry, and other dishes.

Tamale (tah-MAH-lee): A dish of Mexican origin, or variations thereof, usually consisting of spicy seasoned meat and vegetables covered with *masa* (cornmeal) dough.

Tomato paste: A rich, sweet concentrate made from tomatoes that have been cooked for several hours, strained, and reduced. It is available in cans and tubes. **Tomato sauce**, available in cans, is a less sweet, thin tomato purée.

Turmeric (TER-mer-ihk; TOO-mer-ihk): An Indian plant whose powdered rhizomes are used as a condiment.

To whisk: To beat quickly with a light circular motion, using a hand-held metal whisk or rotary beater, or an electric mixer, to incorporate air (fluffiness) into eggs, cream or food mixtures.

White pepper: A less pungent pepper ground from peppercorns from which the outer black layer has been removed, popular for use in light-colored sauces and foods.

White sauce: A sauce made with butter, flour, and milk, cream, or stock, used as a base for other sauces.

Wine

    appellation (ap-peh-LAY-shuhn): A protected name under which a wine may be sold, indicating that grapes used are of a specific kind from a specific district.

    aroma: The smell or fragrance of the wine.

    body: The perception of texture or consistency of a wine in the mouth.

    bouquet (boh-KAY): A unique and complex fragrance that emerges when a wine is fermented and aged.

    complexity: A complex wine has myriad layers and nuances of bouquet and flavor.

    dry: Dry wine has very little or no sweetness. In a *fully dry* wine, all sugar has been converted to alcohol during fermentation. A *medium-dry* wine contains a small amount of sugar, and an *off-dry* wine has the barest hint of sweetness. A wine may be both dry and fruity.

    estate bottled: The winery either owns or controls the vineyard and is responsible for the growing of the grapes used in the wine.

finish; aftertaste: The flavor characteristics of a wine that remain in the mouth and nasal passages after a wine has been swallowed.

nose: A wine's scent or fragrance. "A good nose" means the wine has a fine bouquet and aroma.

sweet: Sweet wine may result naturally from the amount of sugar in the grapes at harvest, or sweetness may be supplemented by the wine maker.

texture: Wine that is perceived as intense and full-bodied, producing a dense impression on the palate that makes the wine seem almost thick.

varietal (vehr-EYE-ih-tl): A wine named for the grape from which it is made. Although one or more grape varieties may be used in making a varietal, by United States law, the wine must be blended from at least 75 percent of the named varietal.

vintage (VIHN-tihj): The year grapes were grown and harvested. In the United States, the wine label may list the vintage year if 95 percent of the wine comes from grapes harvested that year.

viticultural (VIHT-ih-kuhl-cher-uhl) area: A region where grapes are grown.

Worcestershire (WOOS-ter-sheer; WOOS-ter-sher): A rich-bodied, piquant sauce of soy, vinegar, and spices, originating in the borough of Worcester (WOO-ster), England.

Zest: The outermost part of a lemon, lime, orange or other citrus fruit, usually finely grated or shredded, used to add subtle flavor or fruity piquancy to dishes.

Zucchini (zoo-KEE-nee): A variety of elongated, dark green squash. From the Italian *zucca*, "gourd."

INDEX

☆ Cooking With Wine
by Virginia and Robert Hoffman

Eighty-six American winery chefs share 172 of their best recipes for cooking with wine and pairing food with wine in this excellent cookbook. Whether you are a novice or an expert in the kitchen, you'll enjoy these great recipes. But that's not all. You'll also learn how cooking with wine can be good for your health! Included is a glossary of American wines and suggested pairings of wine and food. This bestselling cookbook is considered a classic.

ISBN 0-9629927-3-9, softcover, 206 pages **$15.95**

☆ The Great Little Food With Wine Cookbook, 2nd Edition
by Virginia and Robert Hoffman

There's a lot of information in this cookbook! You'll enjoy excellent recipes by some of America's finest winery chefs, tips on how and where to buy wine, guidelines for selecting wine in restaurants, helpful hints on deciphering wine labels so you know what you're buying, and how to select wines to go with your meals ... and the wines are all American.

ISBN 1-877810-70-3, softcover, 128 pages **$9.95**

☆*Pairing Wine With Food*
by Virginia and Robert Hoffman

In this handy bestselling book, more than 500 foods are paired with American wines. You'll learn where and how to buy wine, how to select wine in a restaurant, and even the right wines to pair with fast- and takeout foods such as nachos, Kentucky Fried Chicken, and pizza. In addition, there's a helpful guide to American wines, and even a Winespeak Dictionary. With this unique book, you'll discover everything you've always wanted to know about pairing wine with food ... and more.

ISBN 1-893718-01-8, softcover, 96 pages **$8.95**

☆*Nancy's Candy Cookbook: How to Make Candy at Home the Easy Way*
by Nancy Shipman

Have fun and save money by making top-quality candy at home. In this step-by-step guidebook, candy specialist Nancy Shipman takes you through the candy-making process and shares her favorite recipes — fudge, divinity, brittles and barks, caramels and nougats, nut clusters, chews, cream, fruit and nut centers, mints and jellies, lollipops, taffy, chocolate pizza, and many more. There are more than 100 excellent candy recipes plus helpful information on types of chocolate and other sweet ingredients, candy-making equipment, dipping and coating, and much more. You'll become an expert candy maker in no time. How sweet it is!

ISBN 1-877810-65-7, softcover, 192 pages **$14.95**

☆ *The Great Turkey Cookbook*
by Virginia and Robert Hoffman

Discover turkey — delicious, versatile, economical, and loaded with health benefits. This collection of 385 recipes puts turkey on the table every day (not just holidays) with its excellent recipes. Appetizers, soups, salads, pastas, sandwiches, chile, fajitas, barbecues and more. Plus, each recipe has a complete nutritional analysis — calories, cholesterol, fat, sodium and protein. A Book-of-the-Month Club selection for two years, more than 100,000 copies have been purchased. Truly a classic cookbook.

ISBN 0-893718-11-5, softcover, 388 pages **$19.95**
ISBN 0-917413-05-9 **CD-ROM** **$14.95**
Turkey Cookbook & CD-ROM package **$29.95**

☆ *The Great Chicken Cookbook*
by Virginia and Robert Hoffman

Chicken is America's favorite! It's tasty, nutritious, convenient and economical. This book contains more than 400 fabulous recipes with timesaving tips and money-saving suggestions for great-tasting leftovers. Quick and easy to prepare, chicken is the perfect choice for the beginning cook and the experienced chef. Each recipe includes complete nutritional analysis and calorie count per serving.

ISBN 0-89594-828-1, softcover, 400 pages **$19.95**

☆ *The Wine-Lover's Holidays Cookbook*
by Virginia and Robert Hoffman

You'll enjoy happier holidays with this timesaving collection of menus, recipes and wine recommendations. There are 13 seasonal holiday menus, with recipes and suggested American wines to accompany them, for Thanksgiving, Christmas, Chanukah, Passover, Easter and the 4th of July. Each is easy to prepare and appropriate for the selected holiday. This charming book is a perfect gift or remembrance for any special occasion.

ISBN 1-893718-03-4, softcover, 144 pages **$9.95**

☆ *The California Wine Country Cookbook II*
by Virginia and Robert Hoffman

Here are 172 exciting recipes from the most creative chefs of the California wine country. Recipes for appetizers, soups, salads, pastas, meats, seafood, poultry, vegetables and desserts — each an exciting addition to your culinary repertoire. Some recipes are quite simple, easy and fast to prepare. Others require more time and effort. All are innovative and will bring the cuisine of the California Wine Country into your home.

ISBN 0-9629927-6-3, softcover, 208 pages   **$12.95**

☆ *The California Wine Country Herbs & Spices Cookbook, New Revised Edition*
by Virginia and Robert Hoffman

Herbs and spices are the theme of this collection of recipes by 96 of the foremost chefs in the California wine country. You'll enjoy 212 of the best recipes that made them world famous for their cuisine. You'll discover exciting new ways to use 37 herbs and spices, how to make your own spice mixes, and how to make herbed and spiced oils and vinegars.

ISBN 0-9629927-7-1, softcover, 240 pages   **$14.95**

☆ *Great Salsas!*
by Virginia and Robert Hoffman

This collection of 96 salsa recipes takes you from mild and mellow to very hot. Discover delicious recipes from Latin America, the Caribbean, Africa, the Far East, and the American Southwest. Each is simple and easy to make ... and guaranteed to tantalize your taste buds. Come with us on a culinary adventure using exotic but easy-to-find ingredients, and enjoy new and exciting flavors, aromas to make your mouth water, and excitement in every taste!

ISBN 1-893718-05-0, softcover, 96 pages   **$7.95**

☆ *Cooking with Chardonnay: 75 Sensational Chardonnay Recipes*
by Barbara and Norm Ray

Chardonnay is one of the most popular white table wines worldwide. Its unique flavors are ideal for drinking and cooking, many excellent vintages are readily available at reasonable prices, and it pairs well with today's lighter cuisine. In this new cookbook you'll enjoy 75 sensational, easy-to-prepare recipes, each of which is flavored with Chardonnay — soups, pastas and grains, meats, poultry, seafood, and desserts. In addition, you'll appreciate the introduction to Chardonnay, helpful guides on how to cook with wine, decipher wine labels, and serve wine, a glossary and pronunciation guide for wine cooking terms ... and more.

ISBN 1-877810-54-1, softcover, 128 pages   **$9.95**

☆ *Cooking with Merlot: 75 Marvelous Merlot Recipes*
by Barbara and Norm Ray

If you, your family, and friends enjoy moderately heavy cuisine with rich wine overtones, think Merlot! This exciting, new cookbook contains 75 marvelous, easy-to-prepare recipes, each of which is flavored with Merlot — soups, pastas and grains, meats, poultry, seafood, and desserts. In addition, there's an introduction to Merlot, helpful guides on how to cook with Merlot, decipher wine labels, and serve wine, a glossary and pronunciation guide for wine cooking terms ... and more.

ISBN 1-877810-53-3, softcover, 128 pages   **$9.95**

☆ ☆ ☆

ORDER

To order Hoffman Press cookbooks through the mail, please complete this order form and forward with check, money order or credit card information to Rayve Productions, POB 726, Windsor CA 95492. If paying with a credit card, you can call us toll-free at 800.852.4890 or fax this completed form to Rayve Productions at 707.838.2220.

We invite you to visit the Hoffman Press website and view our cookbooks at foodandwinebooks.com.

❏ Please send me the following book(s):

Title_____ Price_____ Qty____ Amount _____

Title_____ Price_____ Qty____ Amount _____

Quantity Discount: 4 items@10%;	Subtotal	$_____
7 items@15%; 10 items@20%	Discount	$_____
	Subtotal	$_____

Sales Tax: Californians please add 7.5% sales tax
Shipping & Handling:
Book rate — $3 for first book + $1 each additional
Priority — $5 for first book + $1 each additional

Sales Tax $_____
Shipping $_____
Total $_____

Name _____ Phone _____

Address _____

City State Zip _____

❏ Check enclosed $ _____   Date _____

❏ Charge my Visa/MC/Discover/AMEX $_____

Credit card # _____   Exp. _____

Signature _____ *Thank you!* CWM03